Crossing 24

EMBAR *RACE* MENTS

EMBAR *RACE* MENTS

Daily Embarrassments in Black and White . . . and Color

Kossi Komla-Ebri

Translated by Marie Orton

BORDIGHERA PRESS

Library of Congress Control Number: 2019943037

EDITOR'S NOTE: In Italian, the terms "nero," "negro," and "persona di colore" do not have exact equivalents in English. "Negro" is considered derogatory and racist. Though in most contexts, "negro" is not considered as offensive as the English "nigger," it can sometimes function synonymously. The usage of "di colore" in Italian was originally borrowed from English as an attempt at political correctness, but is now considered a racially charged term. While "nero" is the most accepted racial descriptor, Kossi Komla-Ebri's stories point out that it, too, can often carry a racist taint. For these reasons, we have at times opted to keep the original Italian word in this volume to best reflect the various nuances of meaning.

Printed in the United States.

Published by
BORDIGHERA PRESS
John D. Calandra Italian American Institute
25 West 43rd Street, 17th Floor
New York, NY 10036

Crossings 24
ISBN 978-1-59954-124-2

CONTENTS

ACKNOWLEDGMENTS

ABOUT THE AUTHOR AND TRANSLATOR

INTRODUCTION

I met Kossi Komla-Ebri in 1997. It was June, and I was present at the awards ceremony of the Eks&Tra literary prize for immigrant writers, the first award of its kind in Italy. Kossi is a well-known medical doctor in Northern Italy who left Togo to attend medical school in Bologna, and, to his great surprise, he was one of the prize winners. He arrived accompanied by his wife and his children who had played a major role in his success. They had seen their father scribble away in his spare time and had been the ones to submit his short story. They gave him the great gift of visibility as a writer and the motivation to continue writing.

Writing started as a secondary passion that has, however, turned Kossi into a public intellectual who leverages paradox in his writing and in his political career. He lives in a very conservative region of Lombardy, dominated by a nationalist and populist party known for its misogyny and xenophobia. A few years ago, he became the candidate for a moderate center-left party that had little chance to win the election. Kossi used provocation in order to strategically challenge the conservative apathy of local voters. His round black face dominated the surface of his political posters hanging all over the city, and he designed swag to be distributed at his political rallies. The free gifts were small glass bottles filled with olive oil, meant by Kossi to invoke the name of his coalition party, L'Ulivo. The labels were smaller versions of the election posters sporting a close-up of his face.

Because olive oil is immediately recognizable as a symbol of Italianness and belonging, Kossi's swag thus disseminated his identity as an Italian by superimposing his difference (his face) over a stereotypical Italian product (the olive oil). No matter which political party one belonged to, the reaction to this "gift" was laughter at this playful acknowledgement of what seemed to be a paradox twenty-five years ago: an African-Italian politician. It was a provocative statement coated in humor that transformed him into a local celebrity. It was also the beginning of his career as a writer who embraces humor as a powerful weapon against the troubling and ever-increasing racism in Italy.

Pirandello teaches us that an event provokes laughter when it is a deviation from the norm, a change from what is expected. He uses a rather misogynist example to explain his point, but I usually tell my students that if I were to stumble and fall in front of them during a class, they would probably react instinctively by laughing. It is unexpected and hence comic. However, concern would probably replace that initial laughter. The event would not be comic any more if they were concerned for my well-being. If it then turned out that I was uninjured, my clumsiness could still be humorous when they related my fall later to their friends. Humor is, for Pirandello, an intellectual reaction to the deviation from the norm which is colored with compassion and understanding, and is very different from instinctive laughter. Humor permeates Pirandello's work and exposes the intricacies of life and the human psyche. It is humor that allows writers to create narratives that politically engage the world around us.

Kossi Komla-Ebri's work filters his disappointment with the nationalistic and xenophobic sentiments that dominate the world in which he has lived for longer than three decades through a special kind of humor that powerfully exposes the absurdities of racism. As an educated black man, he is the right individual to show us that racism works as a weapon aimed at any embodiment of difference and crosses all social classes. Kossi's autobiographical narratives examine through humor how he, despite his education and social contributions, is still the target of racist attitudes that attempt to subsume him into the same faceless stereotypes assigned to all black immigrants. It is in fact the difference of the immigrant body that people want to discipline and erase. Bigotry undermines any rational discussion about the economic advantages that migrants bring to a country like Italy.

We do know that there are more Italian citizens leaving Italy and more migrants coming into Italy. Instead of considering this phenomenon as a balancing act, many Italians want to marginalize the latter and make them invisible. However, it has been well-established that migrants bring skills and abilities that would be very useful for the country as a whole. Nevertheless, many who define themselves as Italians see all immigrants homogeneously as "black," no matter the color of their skin. The issue is never the singularity of the individuals who move and

migrate. Dominant discourses treat them as one burdensome mass. For years, politics have increasingly embraced such absurdities. Politics have replicated and disseminated such discourses.

Kossi's narratives intervene in order to interrupt the dominant racist rants through humorous short stories that demand reactions from the readers. And Kossi's stories can't help but provoke a reaction. For example, in the volume's first anecdote, "Hey, *bel negro*, do you want to make a few cents?" the protagonist is in the supermarket parking lot helping his (white) wife load the groceries into the trunk of their car. He then walks back toward the supermarket to return the cart. In Italy, supermarket carts are chained together in order to prevent their theft. A customer inserts a one-euro coin to unlock one cart and the coin is returned when the cart is brought back. On his way back to the carts, the protagonist encounters a native Italian man who motions him that if returns his cart too, Kossi can keep the refund of the one euro.

For the Italian man, interracial couples are an unconceivable concept. Indeed, if they even do exist, then the black member of the couple must be the disadvantaged one, the one inevitably in need of charity. This mindset is the norm for this native Italian man, as he is blind to the pervasive presence of diverse couples in Italy. Kossi's actual situation deviated from this perceived "norm" and makes the story humorous at the expense of the bigoted Italian gentleman. After returning to the car, the protagonist tells his spouse what happened and at subsequent trips to the supermarket, they re-enact together this same moment as a pantomime and inside joke. The humiliation of the original encounter is transformed into humor as it is performed in this space of mutual understanding.

Frequently in these stories, alongside the humor, the protagonists' pain and humiliation remain undiminished. This juxtaposition heightens the feeling of indignation in the reader. Kossi's short stories demonstrate the extent to which diversity is a social construct. In laughing at the racist Italian man at the supermarket, we laugh at socially created prejudices that must be dismantled because they disseminate and perpetrate the marginalization of others. Kossi's sorrow, anguish, and heartache may be coated in humor, but they are there on the page to be understood.

So what are we to do? How can we combat racisms that have become so normalized? This book itself is one answer. Kossi and other writers have given us the tools to fight. Let's take this book and let's circulate it. Let's make sure that all libraries have a copy, and read it to our children and grandchildren. Let's volunteer to read it in schools, in Sunday school, at special events in bookstores. Let's broadcast a new norm grounded in equality and inclusion.

Graziella Parati
Paul D. Paganucci Professor of Italian
Dartmouth College

Preface

Ogni nero che vive in Italia ha un proprio ricco repertorio di «imbarazzismi». Questo fortunato neologismo, ideato da Kossi Komla-Ebri, sta a indicare situazioni che non rientrano nei casi di discriminazione crudele, violenta o quantomeno intenzionale, ma si tratta di episodi di razzismo di piccolo calibro, che avvengono senza che il loro autore se ne sia reso propriamente conto.

L'imbarazzismo, come una gaffe sconveniente, crea disagio. Come un lapsus freudiano, svela giudizi e pregiudizi rimossi. Ma per quanto ciascuno di questi episodi non sia grave, gli imbarazzismi feriscono le loro vittime, perché sono quotidiani e perché illustrano una mentalità diffusa popolata di stereotipi.

Come superarla? Il primo passo per sconfiggere i pregiudizi è quello di saperli riconoscere. Bisogna ammettere che ciascuno di noi ne ha diversi, quindi dobbiamo imparare a vederli e poi essere disposti a rivederli, ampliando le nostre conoscenze e mettendoli a confronto con la realtà dei fatti.

Questa raccolta di aneddoti divertenti, amari e folgoranti ci aiuta a smascherare l'etnocentrismo e gli stereotipi con ironia, un'arma gentile ma efficace contro il razzismo latente.

Il volume del medico-scrittore italo-togolese ci rammenta che dobbiamo fare ancora della strada per costruire una società e una cittadinanza veramente inclusive nei confronti delle minoranze e verso le persone di diversa origine, ma dobbiamo anche constatare che la mentalità sta cambiando ed in parte è già mutata.

La società italiana è in rapida trasformazione: tra i protagonisti delle brevi storie collezionate da Kossi Komla-Ebri — oltre a persone che sono ancora disorientate da un'Italia sempre più meticcia — vi sono molte coppie miste, famiglie adottive, gruppi di amici costituiti da persone di nazionalità diverse. Vi è insomma un Paese per cui nei legami d'affetto e nei rapporti civili il colore della pelle, al pari del colore dei capelli, è solo questione di melanina. Un Paese dove le differenze di ogni consociato sono un potenziale di cui farne tesoro.

On. Cécile Kyenge
Ministro per l'integrazione

Every person of color living in Italy has his or her own rich repetoire of "embar-*race*-ments." This astute neologism coined by Kossi Komla-Ebri serves to describe situations that don't enter into the category of violent, cruel, or even intentional discrimination, but are more those episodes of small-caliber racism, episodes that occur without the perpetrator even realizing it.

An "embar-*race*-ment," like an offensive faux pas, creates uneasiness. Like a Freudian slip, it reveals repressed judgements and prejudices. And while each of these episodes might not be considered serious, "embar-*race*-ments" wound their victims, because they occur daily and because they illustrate a common mentality that is packed with stereotypes.

How can this mentality be overcome? The first step in defeating prejudice is to know how to recognize it. We must admit that each one of us has our own prejudices, and we must therefore learn to identify them and be willing to re-evaluate them, widening our understanding and measuring our prejudices against factual reality.

This collection of comical, acrid, and razor-sharp anecdotes helps us to unmask our ethnocentrism and stereotypes with irony, that gentle but effective weapon against latent racism.

This volume by the Italian-Togolese writer and practicing physician Kossi Komla-Ebri reminds us that there is still a great deal of work to be done in order to construct a society and a citizenry that is truly inclusive of minorities and individuals of different origins, but we must also acknowledge that the current mentality is shifting and to a degree, has already shifted.

Italian society is undergoing a rapid transformation: the protagonists of these short stories collected by Kossi Komla-Ebri stand in contrast to those individuals who are still disoriented by a multicultural Italy. At the same time, there are also many interracial marriages, adoptive families, and groups of friends consisting of individuals from many different nationalities. This is a Nation. Thus, in the bonds of friendship as well as in the interactions in civil society, skin color, just like hair color, must be regarded merely as a question of melanin. A Nation where the differences of every fellow citizen can potentially become a treasure.

The Honorable Cécile Kyenge
Italian Minister of Integration

I. Quotidiani imbarazzi in bianco e nero

I. Daily Embarrassments in Black and White

BEL NEGRO, VUOI GUADAGNARTI 500 LIRE?

Un giorno uscivo dal supermercato con mia moglie, italiana. Avevamo fatto spesa da riempire due carrelli. Dopo aver caricato il tutto nel portabagagli, mia moglie mi spinse i due carrelli per recuperare 500 lire.

M'incamminavo con i miei carrelli, quando sentii alle spalle un – Ssst! – , accompagnato da uno schioccare di dita. Mi girai e vidi un signore sulla cinquantina farmi segno con l'indice di avvicinarmi, e abbozzare il gesto di spingere il suo carrello verso di me. Lo guardai con un'espressione che mia moglie descrisse poi come carica di lampi e fulmini. Comunque il mio sguardo doveva essere stato eloquente, perché lo vidi richiamare il suo carrello e portarselo per conto suo. Senz'altro, visto il colore della mia pelle e il gesto della mia signora di affidarmi i carrelli, il *sciur* aveva fatto la somma: negro + carrelli = povero extracomunitario che sbarca il lunario. Tornando alla macchina, vidi la mia dolce metà, che conoscendo la mia permalosità, si contorceva dalle risate. Mi misi a ridere anch'io. Ora ogni volta che andiamo a fare la spesa, lei mi spinge, ammiccando, il carrello con voce scherzosa:

– Ehi bel negro, vuoi guadagnarti 500 lire?

"HEY, *BEL NEGRO*, DO YOU WANT TO MAKE A FEW CENTS?"

One day I was coming out of the supermarket with my wife, a native Italian. We'd bought enough groceries to fill two carts. After loading everything into the trunk, my wife pushed the carts over to me to take back inside.

I was walking back with both carts when I heard from behind me a "Hey! Hey!" and fingers snapping. I turned and saw a middle-aged man motioning me over with his finger and gesturing that he wanted to push his cart over to me. I looked at him with an expression that my wife describes as "thunder and lightning."

The look must have spoken eloquently because I saw him take his own cart and return it himself.

Obviously, seeing the color of my skin, and seeing how a woman had given the carts to me, the gentleman had made the calculation: "*Negro* + carts = impoverished illegal alien eking out a living."

When I got back to my car, I saw my better half (who knows how touchy I am) in contortions of laughter. I had to laugh, too.

Now every time we go shopping, my wife pushes the cart over to me with a wink and says, "Hey, *bel negro*, do you want to make a few cents?"

LEZIONE DI GEOGRAFIA

Un giorno andavo a scuola di specialità in chirurgia su un treno delle Ferrovie Nord. Ero seduto su quelle poltrone micidiali super riscaldate d'inverno, perciò bisognava discretamente sollevare una natica dopo l'altra per ottenere un po' di sollievo.

La gente, come al solito, occupava prima tutti gli altri posti e solo quando non aveva più altra scelta, disperata veniva man mano a sedersi nei miei paraggi. Un signore sulla sessantina si sedette di fronte a me e vedevo che già si preparava ad attaccare bottone, per cui mi rifugiai dietro il mio libro, per sfuggire al solito interrogatorio poliziesco con l'uso diretto del tu del tipo: – Da dove vieni? Cosa fai? Di che religione sei?

Questa volta, mi trovai di fronte un «attaccatore» coriaceo, che iniziò con:

– Hello! America?

Risposi con un dignitoso silenzio.

– Capire italiano?

Annuii distratto, ma non riuscii a scoraggiarlo.

– Africa?

Annuii di nuovo pazientemente e lui, prendendo la mia apparente rassegnazione come un tacito assenso, proseguì con la sua inquisizione:

– Tu da che paese Africa venire?

Sentii la mia voce rispondere:

– Togo.

In genere a questo punto, c'è chi dice: – Togo? Sì, ma quale paese? Stato? – oppure nasconde la sua ignoranza dietro un – Ah! – d'intendimento, pensando senz'altro ai famosi biscotti.

In fondo hanno ragione: come si fa a raccapezzarsi di fronte a questo continente balcanizzato con tutti quegli statarelli che cambiano nome a ogni starnuto di un nuovo dittatore?

Intanto il viso del mio perspicace aguzzino, dopo aver aggrottato la fronte in un riflessivo e intenso silenzio, s'illuminò di un sorriso di compassione e con infinita sapienza salì in cattedra:

– Ah Togo! Nel tuo dialetto forse dire Togo, ma noi in italiano dire Congo. Tu capire? Congo!!

Certo che avevo capito e. . . grazie per la lezione di geografia!

GEOGRAPHY LESSON

One winter day when I was in medical school, I was riding on a Northern Line commuter train in one of those horrible over-heated cars where the only relief from the temperature is to discretely shift weight from one buttock to the other.

As usual, the passengers took all available places farthest from me. Only when there was no other choice left, out of desperation, someone would come and sit beside me.

An elderly gentleman sat down in the seat opposite. I could see that he wanted to button-hole me, so I took refuge in my book to avoid the ususual police-style interrogation (always using the too familiar "tu" form): "Where're you from?" "What are you doing in Italy?" "What's your religion?"

The man across from me was clearly a veteran button-holer.

He started off with, "Hallo! America?"

I responded with dignified silence.

"You talk my language?"

I nodded "yes," silently but that didn't seem to discourage him.

"You Africa?"

Patiently, I nodded another "yes," and taking my resigned silence as a form of tacit consent, he forged forward with his interrogation:

"Where Africa?"

I heard my own voice responding, "Togo."

Usually at this point most people say, "Togo? Where's that?" or in an effort to hide their ignorance of African geography, they'll give me a vague, "Ah!" of recognition, though we both know they're probably thinking of the Togo brand cookies.

And they're right. How's anyone supposed to keep track of an entire conquistator-ed continent with countries that change names overnight with every overthrown government?

After furrowing his brow in intense silent reflection, the face of my perspicacious tormentor lit up with a smile of compassion as he attempted to explain to me patiently,

"Ah, your dialect maybe say 'Togo,' but Italian say 'Congo.' You understand? You from Congo!!"

Yes, I understood more than you know, and by the way, thank you for the geography lesson!

BABY-SITTER

Un bel pomeriggio di primavera, Charles, un mio amico togolese sposato con una ragazza italiana, portava a passeggio per i giardini pubblici i suoi due figli: quello di due anni per mano e il piccolino di qualche mese nel passeggino.

Incrociarono due signore anziane. Una di loro, mossa a compassione, esclamò:

– *Ohi, por diavül ga tuca fa ül baby-sitter!*

BABYSITTER

My friend Charles from Togo is married to a native Italian woman. One beautiful spring day, he was walking through the park with his two children, holding his two-year old by the hand and pushing the baby in the stroller.

As they walked along, they came across two elderly women, one of whom was clearly moved by compassion when she said, "Oh, that poor young man! He can only find a job as a baby-sitter!"

ORA DI PUNTA

Stavo andando in autobus verso il centro in un'ora di punta. Con un po' di fatica, trovai un posto in fondo, aggrappandomi alla maniglia dell'ultima sedia vicino alla macchina obliteratrice.

A una fermata, un gruppo di chiassosi giovinastri si accingeva a scendere dalla porta posteriore, intralciando e spingendo così quelli che cercavano di salire. Un signore che stava salendo, irritato ed esasperato, li apostrofò: – Scemi! Si scende dal davanti! Idioti! Imbecilli! Selvaggi! Balu. . . ba!

Nel pronunciare quest'ultima parola, il suo sguardo cadde su di me. Nel silenzio gelido passò un angelo con le ali imbrattate di vergogna e le gote rosse d'imbarazzo.

Chissà cosa avranno mai fatto quei. . . Baluba? Non parliamo poi degli Zulù!

RUSH HOUR

I was on a downtown bus during rush hour. With some difficulty, I managed to find standing room at the back near the ticket machine where I could cling to the handle of the seat in front of me.

At one stop, a group of rambunctious Italian teenagers clustered around the back door to get off, tripping and pushing all the people who were making their way onto the bus.

Irritated and exasperated, a gentleman who was desperately trying to get on ranted at their turned backs, "How can you be so stupid?! You get off from the front! You idiots! Imbeciles! Animals! Afri . . . cans!"

Just as he uttered the word, his eye fell on me. In the frozen silence that followed, an angel passed overhead, its wings smeared with shame and its cheeks red with embarrassment.

Who knows what ever became of those "Africans"?

ETNOCENTRISMO

Un giorno in classe, durante un incontro sull'intercultura, chiesi ai ragazzi di darmi una definizione del termine razzismo.

Subito, il più sveglio urlò:

– Il razzista è il bianco che non ama il nero!

– Bene! –, dissi – E il nero che non ama il bianco?

Mi guardarono tutti stupiti e increduli con l'espressione tipo: Come può permettersi un nero di non amare un bianco?

ETHNOCENTRISM

One day when I was visiting a school to give a presentation on multiculturalism, I asked the children to tell me the definition of the word "racism."

The quickest boy called out, "A racist is a white person who doesn't like black people."

"Okay," I said, "What about a black person who doesn't like white people?"

The class looked at me in shock. Their innocent faces seemed to say, "But how could a black person not like a white person?"

IL COLORE DEI SOLDI

Estate, agosto, ferie sospirate dopo un anno passato a lavorare come un . . . negro. Sarebbe, pensava Apélété forte della sua esperienza, più giusto dire: Lavorare come un . . . brianzolo.

Infatti, sposato con una brava brianzola, il nostro amico aveva messo da parte un po' di *danè* e aveva prenotato per telefono una stanza in una pensione in riva al mare. Arrivati a destinazione, mentre lui scaricava i bagagli, la moglie, recuperate le chiavi in reception, salì in camera.

Carico dei bagagli, Apélété si stava avviando verso le scale quando si sentì chiamare dal gestore:

– Ehi tu, dove pensi d'andare?

Al suo sguardo interrogativo e di stupore, il padrone rispose con un linguaggio per sordomuti del genere: Tu non potere andare su!

A questo punto, il nostro amico. . . nero dalla rabbia, si spiegò:

– Ho prenotato qui una stanza più di un mese fa, e infatti mia moglie è appena salita con le chiavi!

– Oh mi scusi –, rispose – l'avevo presa per . . .

E Apélété terminò nella sua mente: Un facchino . . . nero. È proprio vero che la voce al telefono non ha colore, ma di certo neanche i soldi ne hanno.

THE COLOR OF MONEY

Even though in Italian people say, "I was working like a *Negro*," my friend Apèlètè would say that in his experience it's more accurate to say, "Working like someone from Brianzola."

Apèlètè was married to a nice girl from Brianzola, and after working for a solid year without a single day off, he finally had some *danè** set aside and had phoned in a reservation for a vacation spot on the beach.

When they arrived, he unloaded their suitcases while his wife got the keys from the front desk and went up to their room.

Loaded down like a bell boy, Apèlètè started toward the stairs when he heard the manager call out, "Hey, you! Where do you think you're going?"

At Apèlètè's look of surprise and confusion, the manager responded with his most elaborate gestures usually reserved for the deaf, something like, "You no go up stairs!"

At this point, my friend became, as we say in Italian, *black with anger* and concisely replied, "I made this reservation over a month ago. Not two minutes ago you handed my wife the room keys!"

"Oh, excuse me," began the manager, "I thought you were a . . . , a . . . "

Apèlètè mentally finished the thought, a *black* bell boy.

Over the phone, a voice has no race, but evidently money has no race, either.

---

*   "Cash" in Brianzola dialect. Brianza is located in Northern Italy in the Lombardy region, north of Milan.

SCUSI, LEI È ITALIANO?

Finita la scuola d'infermiera professionale, Akolè aveva trovato un posto di lavoro in una casa di cura. Minuta, con modi carini, era molto apprezzata sul lavoro per la sua efficienza e disponibilità.

Eppure quella sera in corsia c'era un paziente che insisteva nel mettere alla prova i suoi nervi.

Non le pesava di certo il fatto che il paziente del letto 124 suonasse a ripetizione, né che s'atteggiasse a onnipotente perché aveva la bocca piena di soldi.

Quello che irritava Akolè era che dalla prima chiamata, appena lei entrò nella stanza, lui, nel vedere la sua faccina abbronzata, indicò la finesta e ordinò:

– Io caldo, tu aprire!

Sbigottita, Akolè andò ad aprire la finestra. Alla seconda chiamata, l'individuo disse:

– Tu, portare me pappagallo per pss! Capito?

Fatto quello che doveva fare, l'energumeno richiamò:

– Io finito, tu portare via pappagallo!

Alla quarta chiamata, l'ostrogoto disse:

– Adesso avere freddo, tu chiudere finestra! Capito? Chiudere finestra!

A questo punto, sull'orlo dell'esasperazione, la nostra amica lo squadrò dall'alto in basso e gli chiese con voce dolciastra e in perfetto italiano:

– Mi scusi, ma lei è italiano? Mi vergognerei da morire se io parlassi così la mia lingua!

E girandosi uscì.

Chissà poi se avrà. . . capito!

A metà corridoio la nostra infermiera si ricordò di non aver chiuso la finestra, ma stranamente il bipede non chiamò più, almeno per quella sera.

Forse aveva capito.

"EXCUSE ME, ARE YOU ITALIAN?"

After finishing nursing school, my friend Akolè found a position working in a nursing home. Very petite and with a gentle manner, she was highly respected for her efficiency and helpfulness.

But one night a certain gentleman put even her patience to the test.

She didn't get upset when the man in room 124 hit the call button continually, or when he acted all-powerful just because he was loaded with money. What really irritated Akolè was how, after seeing her "tanned" face, he spoke to her like this:

"I hot, you open" (turning his finger to the window).

Speechless, Akolè walked over and opened the window.

For his second call, this gentleman said, "You, bring bedpan. I pssssst! You understand?" And after having concluded his physiological business, this fiend in human form called again to inform her, "I done. You take bedpan!"

On his fourth call, this Neanderthal said: "Now cold. You close window. Close window! Get it? Close window!"

Now at her breaking point, our friend looked the man up and down and asked him in honeyed tones and perfect Italian, "Excuse me, sir, but are you Italian? I would be so very embarrassed to speak my own language that way!"

Akolè turned on her heel and left.

Maybe he "got it."

Halfway down the hallway, the nurse in her remembered that she hadn't closed the window, but oddly enough our little Neanderthal didn't call again, at least not that night.

Perhaps he actually did "get it."

PREGASI COLLEGARE LA LINGUA . . . AL CERVELLO

Un giorno, mia moglie e io andammo al supermercato con un mio nipote africano di quattro anni in visita da noi.

Incontrammo una giovane signora, che conoscevamo da almeno una decina d'anni. S'avvicinò e prima ancora di vedere il piccolo esclamò:

– Oh che bello! Com'è cresciuto! È il vostro primo?

Tenete presente che mio nipote era da noi da appena due mesi, e che è nero come il carbone.

In realtà il nostro primo figlio ha ormai nove anni, sua sorella sette, e sono entrambi di colore caffellatte.

A volte basterebbe collegare la lingua. . . al cervello.

"PLEASE CONNECT YOUR MOUTH TO . . . YOUR BRAIN"

One day when my four-year old nephew was visiting from Africa, my wife and I went to the supermarket and took him along.

We ran into a young woman whom we'd known for at least ten years.

She came over and without really looking at the child, gushed, "Oh, what a cutie! And he's gotten so big! Now he's your oldest, right?"

You have to realize that my nephew had been with us for more than two months, he has far darker skin than I do, our oldest was over nine, his sister was seven, and both of them, obviously, are lighter-skinned than I am and darker than their mother.

Sometimes, all you need to do is connect your mouth to . . . your brain.

PUNTO A . . . CAPO

Un giorno, mentre si trovava nel corridoio della corsia dove lavorava come infermiera, Akolè vide arrivare un signore elegante e distinto.

Con premurosa gentilezza, gli andò incontro e gli chiese:

– Mi scusi, posso esserle utile?

Lui rispose con un secco no, e andò diritto verso la dispensa dove le ausiliarie stavano preparando i pasti per i pazienti.

Arrivato lì disse: – Sono il figlio della signora Galimberti del letto 130 che è stata operata stamani. Vorrei parlare con la caposala sulle sue condizioni.

Gli fu indicata la caposala, che era l'infermiera «di colore» che aveva appena sorpassato nel corridoio.

BACK TO THE BOSS

One night when Akolè was working at the hospital, she saw a distinguished-looking gentleman come to the nurses' station.

Very politely she went over to him and asked, "Good evening, may I help you?"

He replied with a brusque "no," and brushed passed her toward the kitchen where the aides were getting the evening meals ready for the patients.

At the kitchen he announced, "I am the son of Mrs. Galimberti in room 130, who was operated on this morning, and I need to speak to the head nurse for the update on my mother's condition."

The aides pointed him to Akolè, the "colored" head nurse he'd just passed in the hallway.

GRANDE CAPO CARLO

Un'estate trovai lavoro come scudiere in una fattoria di cavalli da corsa.

Il fratello del proprietario, l'uomo tuttofare, mi portò a fare il giro delle scuderie. Subito s'informò:

– Tu venire Brasile? (il fratello aveva lì delle tenute).

– No –, risposi – vengo dall'Africa.

– Tu conoscere cavalli?

– Questa è la mia prima esperienza, ma i cavalli mi hanno sempre affascinato.

Intanto eravamo giunti nel box di una bella giumenta rossiccia a cui il proprietario stava dando dell'avena.

Suo fratello disse ancora rivolgendosi a me:

– Tu dare mangiare due volte al giorno cavalli e . . .

A questo punto l'altro l'interruppe dicendo:

– Perché tu parlare così grande capo viso pallido Carlo? Guarda che lui è uno studente al quarto anno di medicina e parla italiano meglio di te . . .

Passò un angelo con le narici palpitanti in groppa a un cavallo impallidito dal disagio.

BIG CHIEF CARLO

One summer I found a job taking care of racehorses at a stable.

The owner's brother worked there as a handyman and squired me around on the grand tour of the place. Inevitably the questions began, "So, you from Brazil?" (He had all the applications right in his hand).

"No," I replied, "I'm from Africa."

"Know anything about horses?"

"This is my first time working at a stable full-time, but I've always loved horses."

By this time, we'd reached the box of a beautiful roan mare that the owner was feeding.

The brother turned to me, and pointing to the horses said, "You, horses. Two times, give food, everyday . . . "

The owner interrupted his brother to ask, "Why you talk like that, oh, big chief pale-face Carlo? You're talking to a fourth-year medical student who speaks Italian better than you do!"

Just then, an angel passed overhead astride a horse, nostrils flaring, pale with embarrassment.

NON C'È PEGGIOR SORDO . . .

Avendo pensato, mia moglie ed io, d'adottare un bambino africano, mi recai al tribunale dei minori per informarmi sulle modalità e l'iter legale da seguire.

Dopo aver girato su e giù per scale e scale, raggiunsi infine l'ufficio predisposto.

Forte delle mie esperienze con la burocrazia, mi accomodai pazientemente su una sedia nel corridoio. Quando arrivò il mio turno, l'impiegata non mi degnò neanche di uno sguardo, intenta com'era a spulciare delle pratiche.

Paziente attesi, fin quando alzò gli occhi su di me:

– Dica!

Iniziai con: – Volevo avere informazioni sull'ad . . .

Ma senza ascoltarmi disse:

– Deve andare in questura.

– Cosa c'entra la questura? Volevo solo. . .

M'interruppe di nuovo, chiamando un altro impiegato dalla stanza accanto:

– Giorgio, vuoi sentire tu cosa vuole questo qua? Io non ci capisco niente!

Feci tre respiri profondi per annegare l'adrenalina che mi stava già inondando tutto il corpo e dissi con calma: – Volevo sapere come fare per l'adozione di uno straniero, perchè . . .

– Deve seguire la via regolare come tutti!

– Appunto, è per questo che . . .

– Perché cerca una corsia preferenziale per essere adottato?

Ci ho messo un po' a fargli capire che non ero io a voler essere adottato, ma che volevo adottare.

Non c'è peggior sordo di chi non vuol sentire.

NO ONE IS DEAFER

My wife and I had been discussing the possibility of adopting a child from Africa, so I went to the Division of Minors at the courthouse to get information about the process and the documents required.

After going up and down multiple staircases, I finally found the right office.

Fortified by my many experiences with Italian bureaucracy, I settled myself into a chair in the hallway to wait patiently.

When my turn finally came, the woman at the desk didn't even bother to look up, intent as she was on shuffling the papers in front of her.

I waited calmly. She finally looked up at me and sighed, "How can I help you?"

I began with, "I am seeking information regarding adoption . . . "

But without even listening to me she said, "You'll have to go to the police station."

"What do the police have to do with it? I only need . . . "

She interrupted me again to call to her colleague, "Giorgio, can you come and talk to this guy? I can't understand a word he says!"

I took three deep breaths to slow my rising adrenaline and said calmly, "I just need information about adopting a foreign child because . . . "

"Well, you'll have to go through the regular channels, like everyone else!"

"Exactly, that's why I'm here and I just . . . "

"Why do you think you'll get preferential treatment to be adopted?"

It took some doing to convince her that I didn't want to *be* adopted, but wanted information *about* adopting.

No one is deafer than one who doesn't want to listen.

CHI HA PAURA DELL'UOMO BIANCO?

Il volo AZ 453 della compagnia Air Afrique proveniente da Parigi per Cotonou, dopo aver fatto scalo ad Abidjan, era stato appena annunciato per l'imbarco immediato al cancello due.

Avevamo priorità noi che eravamo saliti a Parigi. Presi il mio pessantissimo bagaglio a mano con una certa disinvoltura, cercando di far credere che contenesse solo piume.

Davanti a me, uno studente beninese trascinava a fatica un borsone voluminoso, e con evidente fatica si preparava a imboccare la scala del Jumbo.

In quell'istante vidi scendere dall'aereo l'hostess africana, che si sbracciava in direzione dello sfortunato studente per dirgli che quel borsone non poteva essere considerato un bagaglio di cabina.

Ma il nostro arrogante compagno di viaggio non voleva sentire ragioni, e così nacque un'aspra discussione che ci vide tutti spettatori.

L'irremovibile studente si difese aggressivamente dicendo: – Sono salito stamattina a Parigi su questo stesso aereo con questa stessa borsa e nessuno ha trovato da ridire! Siete sempre voi ivoriani a fare storie!

A questo punto la nostra candida hostess nera disse:

– Vuoi che ti chiamo il comandante bianco?

Nello stupore generale passò un angelo nero con pesanti catene alle ali, canticchiando. . . un blues.

"WHO'S AFRAID OF THE BIG WHITE MAN?"

Air Afrique flight AZ 453 from Paris arriving at Cotonou with a stop at Abidjan had just been called to board at Gate 2.

Those of us who had boarded at Paris had priority seating. I nonchalantly picked up my carry-on. It was incredibly heavy, but I casually tried to make it seem like I wasn't carrying anything heavier than feathers.

Just in front of me a student from Benin was struggling with his bursting luggage, sweating as he tried to force his enormous bag up the stairs and onto the aircraft.

Just then I saw an African flight attendant waving her arms at the unfortunate student to inform him that his oversized bag could hardly be considered a carry-on.

Our arrogant fellow-passenger refused to listen to reason and a heated discussion ensued which drew the attention of all the curious passengers.

He was immovable and aggressively defended himself, saying, "I boarded in Paris with this very airline and with this very bag just this morning and no one had a problem with it! It's you people from the Ivory Coast who always want to make problems!"

At this point, our fair flight attendant sweetly offered, "Would you like me to call the captain? He's white."

In this bustle, a black angel with heavy chains all along its wings passed by, humming the blues.

IL TRASLOCO

Cissé accumulava le ferie da due anni per poter passare così due mesi di seguito in Senegal, sua terra natale.

Sulla strada dell'aeroporto di Malpensa, già pregustava, oltre al *tieboudienne* che gli avrebbe fatto trovare sua mamma cucinato con gli ingredienti giusti, le grida di gioia di fratelli, sorelle e cugini, quando avrebbe aperto per loro i suoi due valigioni pieni di regali.

Al check-in, la signorina raffreddò il suo entusiasmo informandolo che le sue valigie pesavano 40 chili e che aveva diritto solo a 20.

La sua gioia si tramutò dapprima in angoscia per sprofondare poi nella più nera disperazione.

Non poteva di certo tornare a casa senza regali dopo tutte le rinuncie che aveva fatto. Sarebbe stata la più cocente delle umiliazioni, perché i regali erano il segno tangibile della sua riuscita in Europa.

Per sua fortuna, una giovane coppia di sposi in viaggio di nozze per Dakar, avendo pochi bagagli si offrì di condividere i suoi chili eccedenti.

La sua euforia fu mitigata dal commento della signorina alla coppia: – Così li abituate male, perché questi qua non viaggiano. . . traslocano.

THE MOVE

Cissè hadn't gone home to Senegal for two years so he could save up enough vacation time to spend two months in his homeland.

On the way to the Malpensa airport in Milan, he was already imagining the cries of joy from his brothers, sisters and cousins when he opened both voluminous suitcases filled with the gifts he'd brought, and tasting his mother's *tieboudienne* made with the "right" ingredients.

At the check-in, the flight attendant chilled his enthusiasm when she informed him that his suitcases weighed 40 kilos and he was only allowed a maximum of 20.

His initial happiness wilted into anguish before passing into the blackest despair.

It was unthinkable to go home without gifts. It would be a burning humiliation. Gifts were the tangible proof that you'd "made it" in Europe.

Fortunately, a pair of young newlyweds was headed for their honeymoon in Dakar. Since they had very little luggage, they offered to divide the extra weight with him.

However, his relief was somewhat marred by the bride's whispered comment to her new husband, "It's not really good to get them used to this kind of thing, because these people don't travel; they move."

MOGLIE E BUOI DEI PAESI TUOI

Quando ero in Francia, un mio professore di fede liberista-avanguardista, che aveva una gran simpatia nei miei riguardi, m'invitava spesso a passare il fine settimana con la sua famiglia. Col tempo, m'ero legato d'affettuosa amicizia ai figli e non perdevamo mai un'occasione per stare insieme.

Una sera, dopo un servizio televisivo sull'intolleranza razziale, il prof, salendo in cattedra, sentenziò: – Non riesco proprio a capire come fa la gente a essere razzista. Vedi, tu qui da noi sei come uno dei nostri figli. Ti trattiamo alla pari, ti parliamo sempre senza atteggiamenti di superiorità, ti facciamo mangiare a tavola con noi. . .

Dentro di me pensai: Tante grazie!

Lui continuava: – Non abbiamo mai tenuto conto del colore della tua pelle. Vedi, noi non siamo razzisti.

Dissi: – Sa, professore, a volte la gente è razzista senza saperlo, almeno finché non è coinvolta in prima persona. Supponiamo per esempio, che m'innamorassi di sua figlia, e, contraccambiato, la chiedessi in sposa, lei cosa direbbe?

Rispose: – Beh. . . questa è un'altra cosa! La nostra discussione si arenò lì.

L'unica cosa strana è che da quella sera non mi ha mai più invitato a casa sua. Chissà mai perché!

MOGLI E BUOI DEI PAESE TUOI *

When I was in France, one of my politically progressive professors took a real liking to me and often invited me to spend the weekend with his family. In time, I became very close to his children and we were always finding things to do together.

One evening after watching a television program together about racial intolerance, my prof got up on his high horse and declaimed, "I completely fail to understand how people can justify being racist. Look at you here with us; you're like one of my own children. We treat you with complete equality, we speak to you without any tone of superiority, we let you eat at our table with us . . ."

I was thinking to myself, "Thank you very much!" while he went on to conclude, "We've never even noticed the color of your skin. As you can see, we're simply not racist."

I asked, "I've noticed sometimes people can be racist without being aware of it, until something happens to them personally. For example, let's suppose I fell in love with your daughter and she fell in love with me and I asked you if I could marry her, then what would you say?"

He replied, "Well! That would be another matter entirely!"

At that point, I gave up on the discussion.

The funny thing was, after that evening, he never invited me to his house again.

Who knows why?

---

*   Italian proverb, "[Obtain] wives and oxen from your own country."

LA VOCE DELL'INNOCENZA

Quando mia moglie e io fummo invitati a una trasmissione televisiva sulla coppia mista, mio figlio di nove anni mi chiese:

– Papà, ma perché devono fare una trasmissione sulla coppia mista? Cosa vuole dire una coppia mista?

Risposi:

– Vedi che papà è nero e la mamma è bianca, noi formiamo una coppia mista. Siccome per la gente è una cosa nuova, vogliono che ne parliamo.

Dopo averci pensato per un po', mi guardò e disse:

– Boh, per me, una coppia mista. . . è un uomo che sposa. . . un robot.

THE VOICE OF INNOCENCE

My wife and I were asked to participate on a television program about "mixed marriages," and my nine-year-old son asked, "Why are they making a television show about mixed marriages? What's a mixed marriage?"

I tried to explain, "Well, daddy is black and your mother is white, so we have a 'mixed marriage.' This is sort of a new thing for people here, so they want your mother and me to come and talk about it."

After thinking about it for a while, my son looked at me and said, "Hm! Well, for me, a mixed marriage would be if a person married . . . a robot!"

BARZELLETTA

– Papà, papà –, disse Fombi tornando da scuola – i miei compagni mi prendono in giro perché sono nero e dicono che in Africa ci sono i cannibali, che la gente va in giro nuda e vive sugli alberi.

Suo padre gli disse:

– Dì pure che è vero: che a casa il nostro albero era vicino a quello dell'ambasciatore italiano, e che era uno spasso vedere la fatica della moglie per salire sul ramo dove passava la notte.

JUST A JOKE

"Dad! Dad!" Fombi said coming home, "The kids at school make fun of me because I'm black. They say that everyone in Africa is a cannibal and the people all run around with no clothes and live in the trees."

His father told him, "Go back and tell them that they're right: back home in Africa, our tree was right next to Italian ambassador's yard. It was always funny to watch his wife try to climb up at night!"

LE RAGIONI DELLA SPERANZA

Salendo sull'autobus, sentii gridare ancora prima di vederlo, un ragazzino di una scuola in cui ero andato a parlare dell'Africa:

– Kossi, ciao Kossi!

Girai la testa in direzione della sua voce e lo vidi strattonato da sua madre che mi squadrò con gli occhi diffidenti, mentre si abbassava farfugliando qualcosa a bassa voce.

Lo sentii ribattere ad alta voce sbigottito:

– Ma, mamma è Kossi!

REASONS TO HOPE

As I got on the bus, even before seeing him, I heard a little boy calling out, "Kossi! Hi! Kossi!" I'd gone to his class at school to talk about Africa.

Turning my head in the direction of the voice, I saw his mother yank him away as she looked me up and down suspiciously and whispered something in his ear through clenched teeth.

I heard him reply out loudly with a look of innocent surprise, "But mama, that really *is* Kossi!"

SINDROME DA VU CUMPRÀ

Tornando da scuola, Gratus passò per il centro per comprare dei quaderni in una cartoleria. Appena entrò con il suo borsone nel negozio, il commerciante gli venne incontro con mani e palme aperte:

    – No grazie, non compriamo niente!

    – Ok! –, disse Gratus – Ma io, posso comprare dei quaderni?

VU CUMPRÀ SYNDROME*

On his way home from the university, Gratus stopped at a downtown stationary store to buy notebooks.

As soon as he walked into the store carrying an over-sized bag, the owner rushed over, showing his empty hands, "No, no, I can't buy anything from you."

"That's fine," said Gratus, "but could *I* buy some notebooks?"

---

* The term was originally aimed at African street vendors in Italy, assumedly deriving from and mocking their inexact Italian ("vuoi comprare," or "do you want to buy?"). The term has come to be applied as an insult to any person of color.

PER CARITÀ . . . !

– Il parroco conosce una signora che ha bisogno di un fisioterapista, ti conviene passare a parlare direttamente con lui.

Gratus s'incamminò per la salita che portava alla dimora del prete.

Arrivato, suonò e vide le tende muoversi alla finestra, ma nessuno aprì. Risuonò. Dei passi affrettati si avvicinarono alla porta socchiusa. Vide spuntare una mano che gli tendeva furtivamente tremila lire.

– No, volevo parlare con il parr. . .

Il resto del suo discorso fu coperto dallo sbattere della porta.

Inorridito, tornò a suonare ancora con insistenza, il dito incollato al campanello.

Dopo un po' la porta si riaprì e svelò il viso della misteriosa mano: era la devota perpetua, che subito gridò:

– Ma insomma, basta per carità! È tutta la mattina che si va avanti così! Cosa vuoi? Un panino?

E al gesto di diniego, replicò:

– Sì, lo so! non con il prosciutto perché non mangi il maiale, vero?

– No, signora! –, urlò disperatamente il nostro malcapitato, e scandendo le parole aggiunse: – So-no-il-fi-sio-te-ra-pi-sta-de-vo-par-la-re-con-il-si-gnor-pa-rro-co.

– Oh mi scusi!

E un angelo carico di una croce pesantissima, girò caritatevolmente il suo sguardo dall'altra parte della strada sussurrando:

– Qualcuno ha detto: Bussate. . . e vi sarà aperto! Non ha detto: Suonate e sarete ascoltati!

"KNOCK AND IT SHALL BE OPENED UNTO YOU"

"The priest knows a woman who needs to find a physical therapist: you should go and speak to the priest directly."

So, Gratus walked up the hill that led to the abode of the aforementioned clergyman.

When he got there, he rang the bell and saw the curtains move at the window, but no one answered the door. He rang again. He heard some hurried steps come to the door, which opened a crack and a furtive hand held out two Euros to him.

"No, I just need to speak to the . . ."

The rest of his sentence was cut off by the sound of the door slamming.

Shocked, Gratus rang again, and again. He practically glued his finger to the doorbell.

A few minutes later, the door opened again, revealing the face that belonged to the mysterious hand: it was none other than the devoted housekeeper who immediately began screaming, "That's enough! Now stop it! You've been carrying on all morning! What do you want? A sandwich?"

When Gratus shook his head no, she countered, "I know, I know, a sandwich without ham because you people don't eat pork, right?"

"No, please, ma'am!" our unfortunate friend yelled in desperation, and added, spelling things out, "I – am – the – phys-i-cal – ther-a-pist. I – was – sent – to – speak – to –the-priest – a-bout – a – pa-tient."

"Oh! I'm sorry . . ."

Just then an angel bearing a heavy cross looked charitably to the other side of the road and whispered, "Some one once said, 'Knock and it shall be opened unto you,' but he never said: 'Ring the bell and you will be heard.'"

QUID PRO QUO

Tornato in Africa per le ferie, un mio vecchio compagno di scuola che lavorava in una falegnameria con il padre, innamorato del design made in Italy, mi parlò del suo desiderio di seguire uno stage in Italia. Non volle aspettare la mia partenza e mi chiese di dargli l'indirizzo di una persona da contattare appena arrivato in Italia. Gli diedi il numero di telefono e l'indirizzo di una famiglia amica, dicendogli che la moglie si comportava con me come fosse la mia seconda mamma. Poiché non sapeva l'italiano, gli dissi di presentarsi solo con queste cinque parole: – *Je suis l'ami de Kossi* (Sono l'amico di Kossi). La signora capiva un po' il francese e il marito lo masticava discretamente.

Arrivato, il mio amico prese il taxi dall'aeroporto alla stazione e qui telefonò dicendo: – *Je suis l'ami de Kossi*.

In un primo tempo la signora pensò che fossi di ritorno, in vena di scherzi. Ma il ripetitivo *Je suis l'ami de Kossi* la convinse presto del contrario, e dopo incroci telefonici con il marito, si mise d'accordo con l'amico per andare a prenderlo in stazione.

Quando arrivò, la signora non si pose il problema di come riconoscere *l'ami de Kossi*. Senza alcun dubbio doveva essere quel signore abbronzato, elegante, con la sua valigia ventiquattr'ore.

Dal lato suo, il mio amico, vedendo avvicinarsi a lui una signora bionda, elegante e carina, che lo fissava con insistenza, e con un sorriso aperto, equivocò sulle sue intenzioni e si girò da un'altra parte.

Eppure, si diceva la signora, non poteva essere che lui! Ma avvicinandosi, vide quest'ultimo girare di nuovo la testa con un po' di sufficienza.

Quanto al mio amico, benché sicuro del suo charme, non riusciva a raccapezzarsi di questo successo così immediato, del suo fascino esotico sulle italiane.

Ed è con un po' d'irritazione che vide la signora abbordarlo con decisione con queste parole:

– *Je suis l'ami de Kossi*.

A questo punto scoppiarono tutti e due in fragorose risate.

Riconosco tuttavia d'essere stato causa di questo quiproquo, in quanto non essendo abituato a dare peso alle apparenze e parlando della

QUID PRO QUO

When I was back in Africa for a visit, one of my old friends from grade school who worked in his father's carpentry business told me how he had fallen in love with any design "Made in Italy." He told me all about his dream of finding a design internship in Italy. Not wanting to wait until I went back to Italy, he asked me to give him the address of someone he could contact as soon as he got to Italy. I gave him the phone number of a family of close friends, and told him that the wife had always been like a second mother to me. Because my friend didn't speak any Italian, I told him he could introduce himself with five words: "*Je suis l'ami de Kossi*" ("I'm a friend of Kossi"). The mother in the family understood French and the father spoke a little, too.

Once he got to Italy, my friend took a taxi from the airport to the train station, where he called my friends and said, "*Je suis l'ami de Kossi.*" At first the family thought that I was back in town and felt like joking around, but my friend's insistent, "*Je suis l'ami de Kossi, je suis l'ami de Kossi,*" finally convinced the mother that wasn't the case. After a flurry of phone calls with the husband, she told my friend she would come and get him from the station.

When she got there, the mother of the family had no problem picking out "*l'ami de Kossi.*" No doubt he was the dark, well-dressed gentleman carrying a briefcase.

My friend, on the other hand, seeing an attractive blonde woman staring insistently at him and approaching him with an engaging smile, misunderstood her intentions and turned away abruptly.

"But that has to be him!" she thought.

Yet when she approached again, he turned away again with increasing irritation.

As for my friend, though he was quite convinced about how charming he was to the ladies, was mystified by this indication of his instant appeal, some exotic fascination that Italian women had for him.

So he was actually growing quite irritated when the woman tried to hit on him with these words, "*Je suis l'ami de Kossi.*"

That made them both break out in hysterical laughter.

I realize that I was the one at fault for this quid pro quo. Because

signora come di una seconda mamma, non mi era sembrato importante precisare quanto fosse giovane e carina. . .

Un angelo nero perse un pregiudizio nel rumore di due risate.

I usually don't give much importance to appearances, when I told my friend about my "Italian mother," it didn't occur to me to tell him how young and pretty she was.

A black angel passed overhead, losing a prejudice in the sound of their laughter.

OGNI PAESE . . . È MONDO!

Una signora era appena tornata dal suo viaggio in Kenya, dove aveva alloggiato in un albergo della linea Italian style, esclusivo per turisti italiani, con cuoco italiano, personale e guida locale parlanti italiano. Disse incontrando Amavi:

– Jambo! Jambo!

Di fronte allo sguardo interrogativo di Amavi, gli chiese meravigliata:

– Come, lei non parla lo swahili?

– No signora, io parlo l'ewe, lei no?

THINGS ARE THE SAME ALL OVER

An Italian woman had just returned from her trip to Kenya where she had stayed in a hotel "Italian style," exclusively for Italian tourists with an Italian cook and a local, personal tour guide who spoke Italian.

When she returned to Italy, and happened to see my friend Amavi, her first words were, "Jambo! Jambo!"

The woman noticed Amavi's confused look and asked in surprise, "What, don't you speak Swahili?"

"No, ma'am. I speak Ewe, don't you?"

EUFEMISMO

Stavo confezionando un gesso dietro il paravento, quando bussarono.
Pregai l'infermiera di vedere chi fosse quel paziente . . . impaziente.

– Mi scusi infermiera –, disse una signora – non c'è quel dottore?

– Quale dottore signora?

– Sa. . . –, disse esitante – hmm . . . quello con gli occhiali.

– Sono in tanti con gli occhiali – rispose perfidamente l'infermiera.

–Quello . . . quello di . . . –, disse la signora, annaspando per trovare
il termine più appropriato.

– Quello . . .? –, chiese impietosamente l'infermiera. E la signora
in apnea disse:

– Quello di . . . quello un po' . . . insomma quello . . . negrettino!

– Lei cerca il dottor Kossi?

– Appunto! –, rispose con evidente sollievo.

– Se vuole aspettare un attimo, sta visitando.

– Grazie.

Io intanto, dall'alto dei miei cento chili, pensavo: Cara signora mia,
definire uno della mia stazza un negrettino. . . è davvero un eufemismo!

EUPHEMISMS

One day at work I was behind a screen putting a cast on a patient when I heard someone knock. I asked the nurse to go and see who the "impatient patient" was.

"Excuse me, nurse," a woman's voice asked, "is that one doctor in?"

"Which doctor is that?"

"Oh, you know," she said hesitantly, "ummm . . . the one . . . the one with the glasses."

"Most of them wear glasses."

"I mean the one . . . oh, the one . . ." floundered the woman, groping to find an appropriate adjective.

"Yes, the one . . . ?" the nurse prompted uncharitably.

Charging ahead breathlessly, she blurted, "The one . . . the one that's a little . . . well, you know, the little *negrettino!*"

"You mean you're looking for Dr. Kossi."

"Yes!" she said with evident relief.

"If you could please wait a moment, he's currently with a patient."

"Thank you."

As I stood there, looking down at the profile of my 220 pounds, I thought, "My dear lady, defining anyone in my weight class as a 'little' *negro* can only be considered a euphemism."

VU CUMPRÀ MANIA

Quando Kuma si recò con la sua adorata Serena in Sardegna per conoscere i futuri suoceri, lei lo portò ad assaporare la tiepida brezza salmastra della sera in spiaggia. Mentre Kuma apriva il borsone per estrarne il telo da mare per sdraiarsi, gli si avvicinarono due amabili signore che con sollecitudine chiesero:

– Non hai qualche braccialetto o collanina da vendere?

VU CUMPRÀ MANIA

When Kuma went to Sardenia with his fiancé Serena to meet his future in-laws, she took him to the beach one evening to enjoy the warm salty breeze of the sea at sunset.

Just as Kuma opened his bag to pull out his beach towel and stretch out, two friendly women came over to him and asked patronizingly, "Aren't you selling any bracelets or necklaces?"

D'USO COMUNE

Il sindaco di una grande città del nord Italia, in un discorso ufficiale, definì con il termine *vu cumprà* i venditori ambulanti senegalesi.

Qualcuno obiettò che la parola era offensiva e carica di significato dispregiativo.

Il primo cittadino ribatté che si trattava di una polemica pretestuosa in quanto ormai *vu cumprà* era una parola d'uso comune.

Quando chiesero a un mio amico giornalista senegalese cosa ne pensasse, rispose:

– Dite a quel sindaco che è un cretino! Tanto, cretino è ormai una parola d'uso comune.

COMMON USAGE

While making an official statement, the mayor of a major city in Northern Italy referred to all Senegalese street vendors with the offensive term "vu cumprà."

Someone objected that the term carried a deeply pejorative meaning.

As "city father," the mayor defended himself by saying that any discussion of terminology would merely be arguing semantics because nowadays "vu cumprà" was in common usage.

When asked what he thought of the mayor's response, my Senegalese friend who is a journalist replied, "You can tell the mayor that he is an idiot! After all, nowadays 'idiot' is a term in common usage."

CULTURE ... ALTRE

Questa storia mi è capitata con un mio amico tedesco, Michael, ai tempi dell'università.

Michael si diceva avido di conoscere altre culture e imparare cose nuove. Così un'estate lo invitai a casa mia in Togo. All'inizio era entusiasta di tutto, ma dopo due giorni si chiuse in un mutismo totale.

Alla mia reiterata insistenza di conoscere la causa di questo pesante silenzio che stava minando la nostra amicizia, sbottò nervosamente:

– Ma perché camminate così e fate tutto con tanta lentezza? Perdete troppo tempo! Perché mangiate tutti assieme nello stesso piatto? Non è igienico! Perché nei vostri cortili c'è sempre tanta gente? Così non c'è privacy! Perché non fate come noi, noi ... noi ...

Cercai di spiegargli che questo nostro modo di mangiare diverso, di camminare diverso, di vestirsi diverso erano appunto gli elementi della nostra cultura e che, rifiutando questo, in qualche modo rifiutava la mia cultura.

Allora non riusciva a capirmi. Solo al suo ritorno Michael mi dichiarò abbracciandomi all'aeroporto:

– Sai, Kossi, ho imparato una cosa importante in Africa: io sono europeo.

– Sì caro Michael –, avrei voluto dirgli: Stai ancora sbagliando. Tu sei tedesco!

OTHER CULTURES

This happened when my friend from Germany, Michael, and I were going to college.

He told me that he was eager to encounter other cultures and learn new things. So one summer I invited him to spend the summer with me at my home in Togo. At first, he seemed excited about everything, but after two days in Togo he withdrew into total silence.

My insistent questions about what was bothering him, and the fact that his stony silence was affecting our friendship finally made him burst out, "Why do you walk like that and do everything so slowly? You're wasting time! And why do you all eat from the same plate? That's not hygienic! Why do you always have so many people on your patio? There's never any privacy! Why don't you do things like us . . . like us . . . like us?"

I tried to explain to him that *our* ways of walking, of eating, of dressing were the very differences that made *our* culture, and by rejecting them, he was essentially rejecting my culture.

He couldn't understand what I meant. It was only when he was about to leave, as he hugged me good-bye at the airport that Michael told me, "You know Kossi, I learned something important in Africa. I learned that I am a European."

"You know, Michael my friend," I should have told him, "you're wrong: you're not just a European, you're a German."

INTERCULTURA E VERGOGNA

La signora maestra con assoluta certezza affermò:

– Vede, in classe abbiamo un ragazzino di colore e vorremmo approfittare della sua presenza per fare dell'intercultura. Ma. . . niente da fare. L'altro ieri gli ho chiesto di dirci una parola in africano e lui, silenzio totale.

Concluse sagacemente:

– Secondo me si vergogna delle sue origini!

Può anche darsi, ma cara maestra mia, mi dica lei una parola in europeo!

MULTICULTURALISM AND SHAME

The teacher staunchly declared, "You see, children, here in class we have a little colored boy and we should take advantage of his presence to become more multicultural, but, unfortunately, that's not going to work. Just yesterday I asked him to say a few words to me in African, and he was totally silent."

She concluded solemnly, "I'm afraid that he's ashamed of his own origins!"

That may be, my dear teacher, but in the meantime could you say a few words for me in "European?"

INDOVINA CHI VIENE A CENA

Ormai lo so:

– Qui non si può far visita all'ora di pranzo o di cena se non sei invitato, altrimenti vai a finire con una rivista in mano sul divano o peggio a dialogare con un televisore acceso perché non hanno scongelato la bistecca per te. Se ti invitano poi, devi portarti dietro dei fiori per la signora oppure un pacchetto di cioccolatini, pasticcini per i bimbi, o una bottiglia di vino o di liquore per il signore.

Cercai di spiegarlo al mio amico ivoriano Daouda. Spero che mi abbia capito.

– Il guaio con gli africani – mi confidava una mia amica italiana – è che se ne inviti uno, non solo non porta niente, peggio c'è il rischio che si porti dietro un amico.

"GUESS WHO'S COMING TO DINNER?"

I get it.

In Italy, you can't just drop by at dinnertime if you're not invited. If you do, you'll find yourself sitting alone on the couch with a magazine and having a conversation with the T.V. because they didn't defrost a steak for you.

If you do get invited, then you have to bring flowers for the lady of the house, or a box of chocolates, some toys or pastries for the children, and a bottle of wine or liquor for the husband.

I've tried to explain it to my friend Daouda from the Ivory Coast. I hope he understood.

An Italian friend later confided in me, "The trouble with Africans is that if you invite one, not only do they come empty-handed, there's the even greater risk that they'll bring along a friend."

IDENTITÀ

Appena sposati, le *amiche* di mia moglie erano davvero incuriosite dalla nostra coppia. Di certo per loro aver sposato un negro era davvero una cosa . . . strana.

– Cosa mangia? –, le chiesero alcune senz'altro agghiacciate al pensiero di un menù a base di serpente affumicato o di ginocchio d'elefante bollito.

– Chissà come verranno fuori i vostri figli! –, esclamò un'altra di fede milanista tormentata all'idea di una generazione a strisce tipo zebra-Juventus.

L'intellettuale del gruppo si contorceva la mente nel dilemma amletico: – In chi e in che cosa si identificheranno i vostri figli?

Oh Dio! Finora per i miei figli sono il loro papà e mia moglie è semplicemente la loro mamma.

Credo che loro si sentano ormai . . . cittadini del mondo.

IDENTITY

Just after we were married, some *friends* of my wife were incredibly curious about us. For them, evidently, marrying a black person would be, well, strange.

"What does he eat?" they asked my wife, somehow fixated on the idea that the staple of our diet had become smoked snakes or boiled elephants knees.

"But what on earth will your children look like?!" another friend worried. She was an avid supporter of Milan's soccer team, and was probably tormented by the image of a future generation of children that were zebra-striped like the Juventus jerseys.

The intellectual of the group bent her mind toward the Hamletian dilemma, "But with what and with whom will your children personally identify?"

Good grief! My children have always known that I'm their father and that my wife is their mother.

I believe my children now feel they are citizens of the world.

II. Più quotidiani imbarazzi
in bianco e nero . . . e colore

II. More Daily Embarrassments
in Black and White . . . and Color

QUESTIONE DI QI

Quando mi fu concessa la cittadinanza italiana, il maresciallo della stazione dei carabinieri della zona, nel complimentarsi con me, puntualizzò:

– Ora dovrà fare il servizio militare.

– Maresciallo, io sono contro la guerra... tutte le guerre!

– Ma no! È solo pro forma. Vista la sua età, dovrà solo presentarsi per la visita.

Tirai un profondo sospiro di sollievo e il giorno prestabilito mi recai alla caserma militare.

Mi trovai un po' a disagio in mezzo a tutti quei giovinastri con la peluria nascente che purtroppo dovevano assolvere quest'assurdo impegno: imparare a uccidere altri esseri umani.

Fummo subito introdotti da un giovane militare (sergente, non ricordo) in una grande aula per rispondere a un questionario.

Durante l'appello ci minacciò: – State buoni e calmi se no ve la vedrete con me!

Con pazienza compilai l'assurdo questionario a risposte multiple, che mi chiedeva cose del tipo: *Hai mai sentito una voce che ti diceva: – Alzati e vai a salvare la patria? –*, oppure: *– Credi che senza la paura di una sanzione, la gente sarebbe naturalmente onesta? –*, e altre domande ancora più allucinanti.

Il giovane ritirò il compitino per portarlo alla psicologa.

Mentre eravamo tutti in fila, con addosso solo gli slip e in attesa della visita medica per la palpazione, mi sentii chiamare dalla voce tonante del nostro giovane militare:

– Koossi Koomm...

– Sono io –, risposi per evitargli di torturare impietosamente il mio cognome.

– Si risponde: presente!

– Presente! –, ripetetti docilmente.

– Cosa c'è? –, chiesi incamminandomi dietro di lui in quella tenuta.

– La psicologa vuole vederti!

– Ah?

– Sì, perché . . . sicuramente tu non conoscere bene l'italiano: hai risposto a caso ed è venuto fuori che tu avere un QI superiore alla media . . . quindi devi rifare il questionario.

I. Q. TEST

When I received my Italian citizenship, the marshall of the local carabinieri station congratulated me and also informed me, "Of course now you'll have to complete your year of military service."

"But Marshall, I'm opposed to war, all wars!"

"Don't worry! It's just pro forma. At your age, you just go down to the military base and fill out a form."

I let out a deep sigh of relief. On the appointed day, I presented myself at the military base.

I felt a little uncomfortable sitting there with all the potential recruits who were just getting their first peach fuzz, yet unfortunately had the absurd assignment of learning how to kill people.

We were directly introduced to a young soldier (sergeant something? I don't remember), who took us into a large room to take a test.

During the roll call he threatened, "Shut up and sit still, or you'll answer to me!"

I patiently answered the ridiculous multiple-choice questions that asked things like, "Have you ever heard a voice inside telling you, 'Go and save your country?'" or "Do you believe that without the threat of punishment, people would naturally be honest?" and even more alarming questions.

A young soldier collected our "exams" and took them to the psychologist.

While we were standing in line in our underwear waiting to be squeezed in the medical exam, I heard my name being called in the thunderous tones of a young sergeant, "Koosssi Kooomm . . ."

"That's me," I shot back, to avoid the merciless torturing of the pronunciation of my last name.

"You have to say, 'Here.'"

"Here," I added compliantly.

"What's going on?" I asked, as I followed the uniform in front of me.

"The psychologist wants to see you."

"Really?"

"Yes, because . . . obviously you no speak Italian good and you just filled in your test randomly. Test came back, you have above average I.Q., so . . . you have to retake the test."

– Ah! Bene! –, dissi, e per un attimo mi parve di scorgere nel cortile un angelo nero sghignazzante, in gonnella di paglia, con un ossicino nel naso e una lancia in mano, che ballava a suon di tam-tam attorno a un pentolone sul fuoco.

Just then from the corner of my eye, I seemed to notice a black angel in the courtyard laughing scornfully, wearing a grass skirt, with a bone through its nose and a spear in hand, beside a smoking pot over a flame, dancing to the sound of a tam-tam.

DELLA . . . BRAVURA

– Mi scusi signora, i ragazzi sono fratello e sorella? –, chiese un'anziana signora a mia moglie, che passeggiava con i nostri due figli.

– Sì.

– Oh! Ma com'è stata brava ad adottarli assieme!

GOODNESS

"Excuse me, but those children, are they brother and sister?" an elderly woman asked my wife when was taking our children for a walk.

"Yes."

"Oh! It was so good of you to adopt them both together."

!!!

PERMALOSITÀ . . . NERA

Due amici senegalesi (Ndiaye e Sebé) s'incontrarono sul binario nove della stazione centrale:

– *Na nga def?* (Come stai?)

– *Ma ngi fi rek.* (Esisto sempre!)

– *Na ka liguey bi.* (Come va il lavoro?)

– *Alamdoulai.* (Tutto ok!)

Mentre si scambiavano i saluti, Sebé notò con la coda dell'occhio una signora di mezza età che continuava a guardarli con insistenza.

– Hai visto come ci guarda quella *tubab*?

– Chi?

– Quella lì seduta sulla panchina!

– Ma no!

– Ma sì! Ci guarda come se non avesse mai visto un negro!

– Lascia perdere, è una tua impressione!

– Eh no! Adesso vado a chiederle se non ha mai visto un negro in vita sua!

– Dai Sebé, lascia perd . . .

Ndiaye non fece in tempo a bloccare l'amico, che in due falcate quello raggiunse la signora investendola con:

– Cos'ha da guardarci così? Non ha mai visto un negro?

– Mi scusi... non intendevo offendervi! Sa, mia figlia è fidanzata con un senegalese e mi sembravate due amici loro che sono venuti a trovarci l'altra sera!

L'angelo nero con lunghe braccia ciondolanti rimase lì a bocca aperta . . . sfoggiando bianchissimi denti.

HYPERSENSITIVITY

Two Senegalese friends, Ndiaye and Sebè, met at track nine at the downtown train station.

"Na Nga def?" (How are you?)

"Ma ngi fi rek." (I'm hanging in there.)

"Na ka liguey bi." (How's work?)

"Alamdoulai." (It's all right).

From the corner of his eye, Sebè noticed that an older woman was staring at them.

"Have you seen how that *tubab* is staring at us?

"Who?"

"That lady sitting on the bench."

"Oh, she is not!"

"Oh, she is, too! She's looking at us like she's never seen a black person before!"

"Forget it. You're just imagining things."

"I am not! I'm going to go right over to her and ask her if she's ever seen a black person before in her life!"

"Come on, Sebè, drop it."

Ndiaye wasn't fast enough to stop his friend. The next second, he'd gone over to the woman and hit her with, "Why you are staring at us? Haven't you ever seen a black person before?"

"I beg your pardon. I didn't mean to be rude. You see, my daughter is engaged to a Senegalese man, and you seemed like two of their friends who came over to our house the other night."

" . . . "

Just then, a black angel with long dangling arms stood there speechless . . . with perfectly white teeth.

AGGIUNGI UN POSTO A TAVOLA

La famiglia di un'amica di Marzia, una donna molto, molto religiosa, vedeva spesso a messa un giovane «di colore» in piedi in fondo alla chiesa. Era ormai dicembre e i genitori della sua amica pensarono che sarebbe stato un gesto di cristiana carità invitare a pranzo quel ragazzo qualche giorno prima di Natale.

Vedendolo sempre solo, in disparte, avevano concluso che si trattava di uno di quei ragazzi africani venuti a frequentare la loro prestigiosa università, e che quindi avrebbe sicuramente passato le feste di Natale pressoché solo.

Lo invitarono così a pranzo e lui accettò di buon grado. Quando furono tutti seduti attorno al tavolo, gli chiesero da dove veniva e cosa faceva in Italia. La risposta, semplice e diretta, fu: – Sono l'ambasciatore della Guinea-Bissau in Italia.

L'amica di Marzia non riuscì a contare i minuti di imbarazzatissimo silenzio che seguirono quell'inattesa rivelazione.

AN EXTRA PLACE AT DINNER

Marzia is a devoutly religious woman. Her friend's family often noticed a young man "of color" at mass standing in the back of the church. Since it was December, her friend's parents thought it would be an act of Christian kindness to invite the young man to dinner some evening around Christmas.

They noticed that he always came alone and sat alone, and they "understood" that he must be one of those young Africans who came to study at their prestigious university, which meant that he would certainly be spending the holidays more or less alone.

They invited him to dinner and he graciously accepted. When they all sat down to dinner, they asked him where he came from and what he was doing in Italy. His answer was direct and without any hint of reproof, "I am the ambassador to Italy from the Republic of Guinea-Bissau."

Marzia's friend didn't count how many minutes of embarrassed silence followed this surprising revelation.

BADI . . . BENE O LA SINDROME DA BADANTE

Ribka si recò all'ASL per compilare le schede d'iscrizione al servizio sanitario.

L'impiegata le chiese nome e cognome per trascriverli. Giunta alla voce professione, scrisse spontaneamente: domestica.

– Perché ha scritto domestica?

– Perché, che lavoro fai?

– Sono una scrittrice, attualmente ricercatrice presso la vostra Università.

– . . . Che sbadata!

WOES OF AN ATTENDANT TO THE ELDERLY

Ribka went to the Local Health Authority Office to fill out the required application for receiving medical services.

The person at the desk asked her first and last name, and began filling in the form for her. In the slot marked, "Profession," the worker automatically wrote down, "maid."

"Why did you write down 'maid'?"

"Because, well, what is your occupation?"

"I'm a writer and am currently employed at your university as an instructor."

"   . . .   "

Whoops!

LA BUONA EDUCAZIONE

Ora di punta sull'autobus.

Daouda, di ritorno dal lavoro, si sedette sfinito sulla sedia vicino alla macchina obliteratrice e chiuse gli occhi per rilassarsi. Alla fermata successiva, un'arzilla vecchietta appena salita gli piombò addosso con veemenza, prima ancora che lui si accorgesse della sua presenza, e l'apostrofò in modo aggressivo, con voce alta e stridente:

– Giovanotto! Nel suo paese cosa si fa quando una persona anziana sale sull'autobus?

– Ce la sbraniamo, signora!

Tutti scoppiarono a ridere.

GOOD MANNERS

Rush hour on the bus.

Coming home from work exhausted, Daouda found a seat near the ticket machine and closed his eyes to relax. At the next stop, a sprightly little old lady got on, planted herself directly in front of him, and before he was even aware of her presence, she attacked him in a shrill, angry voice, "Young man! In your country what do people do when an elderly person gets on a bus?"

"We chop them up for dinner."

Everyone on the bus burst out laughing.

ASPETTANDO L'AUTOBUS

Un'amica eritrea e un signore italiano aspettavano tutt'e due l'autobus n° 25.

– Quest'autobus è sempre in ritardo!

– È vero! Meno male che oggi non piove.

E per venti minuti andarono avanti a parlare del tempo e della scomparsa delle mezze stagioni, finché lui le chiese:

– Lei parla italiano?

Lei rimase esterrefatta.

– Mi scusi, ma in che lingua abbiamo parlato fino adesso?

WAITING FOR THE BUS

An Eritrean friend and an Italian gentleman were both waiting for the 25.

"This bus is always late!"

"I know! Thank goodness it's not raining."

For another twenty minutes they went on talking about the weather and the end of summer when the gentleman asked, stunned, "So, you speak Italian?"

"Well, sir, what language have we been speaking up 'til now?"

IL PANE DELLA PADRONA

Suzanne, salvadoregna, felicemente sposata con un italiano, è supercoccolata dai familiari di lui.

Basti pensare che per non farle sentire la nostalgia di casa, non perdevano l'occasione di cucinare cibi latino-americani o di parlarle in spagnolo.

Una mattina lei decise di iniziare ad arrangiarsi da sola, e uscì per comprare il pane nel negozietto a pochi isolati da casa, dove era solita andare la suocera.

Quando giunse il suo turno, puntando l'indice verso lo scaffale, disse:

– Vorrei quattro pezzi di quel pane.

La negoziante, squadrando la sua faccina minuta, i suoi dolci e timidi occhi lievemente a mandorla rispose:

– Guarda che quello non è il pane che compra la tua padrona!

THE BOSS' BREAD

Suzanne is from El Salvador, happily married to an Italian man and is beloved and completely coddled by his family.

For example, to keep her from feeling homesick, her husband's family tried to cook Latin American food and speak in Spanish every chance they could.

One morning she decided to start doing things on her own. She went out to buy bread at the bakery nearby where her mother-in-law always shopped.

When it was her turn, she pointed toward the shelves and told the woman behind the counter, "I'd like four pieces of that bread, please."

The salesclerk looked her up and down, noted her delicate features, her gentle and timid slightly slanted eyes, and replied, "Look, that's not the bread that your boss always buys!"

NESSUNO

Ribka era sola in ufficio. Le sue due colleghe italiane erano in pausa caffè. Una signora entrò senza bussare. Ribka sentì il suo sguardo laser trapassarla per vagare contrariato sulle sedie vuote.

– Dica signora!

– Non c'è nessuno?

– Come?

– Non c'è nessuno?

Ribka pensò tra sé: E io chi sono? Una sedia, un tavolo?

Poi le domandò:

– Mi dica signora, come la vuole? Bionda? Rossa? Bruna?

Un angelo ciclope, l'occhio trafitto d'imbarazzo, smise d'invocare Nessuno.

NO ONE

Ribka was alone in the office. Her two Italian colleagues were on their coffee break. A woman entered without knocking. Ribka felt the woman's laser gaze pass her over and meander grumpily around the empty chairs.

"May I help you?"

"No one's here?"

"I beg your pardon?"

"No one's here?"

Ribka thought to herself, "What am I? A chair, a table?" then she asked, "How would you like the somebody to be? Blonde? Redhead? Brunette?"

A Cyclops angel passed overhead, its eye pierced by embarrassment, and ceased to call out No one.

LA GAFFE

Il mio amico nigeriano Dan fa l'ingegnere e vive in Toscana. Tempo fa, ebbe un incarico dal tribunale come consulente tecnico per una perizia. Uno dei consulenti di parte era un ingegnere livornese di mezza età. I livornesi sono singolari per la loro spontaneità (talvolta ironici) e si dice (alla faccia dei luoghi comuni) che siano abituati relazionarsi agli altri senza pregiudizi.

Per farla breve, la prima sessione di lavoro avvenne dopo un contatto telefonico. Il nostro livornese sentì il suo buon italiano con accento toscano e quindi non si accorse di nulla.

Due giorni dopo s'incontrarono nell'ufficio di Dan. Si presentarono e parve tutto ok: si trovò davanti un giovane architetto di colore e, da buon livornese, riuscì a gestire la sorpresa egregiamente.

Dan, da parte sua, cercò di metterlo a suo agio trattando argomenti sociali, politici e, ovviamente, parlando di calcio.

L'ingegnere livornese volle sapere dove aveva conseguito la laurea e altri dettagli sulle sue esperienze professionali. Rassicurato, si prodigò in complimenti e non nascose il suo stupore per la sua conoscenza delle tematiche italiane.

Ormai in confidenza, l'ingegnere si sfogò su quanto la sinistra avesse rovinato questo paese (credeva molto più nella meritocrazia che nell'uguaglianza e negli stessi diritti per tutti). Non poteva di certo sapere che Dan era assessore in un'amministrazione di sinistra.

Ormai lanciato, continuò dicendo quanto bisognasse lavorare in Italia per poter pagare le tasse.

– Ti fai un culo come un negro e non riesci a sbarcare il lunario, è inaccettabi . . .

Si accorse della gaffe. Dan si misi a ridere . . .

Lui, in crisi . . . nera.

FAUX PAS

My Nigerian friend, Dan, is an architect and lives in Tuscany. A while ago, he had a contract from the Courthouse as a technical consultant to make an estimate. Another of the consultants was a middle-aged engineer from Livorno. The Livornese are known for being witty, frequently ironic, and it's said that (so much for sterotypes) they treat others without prejudice.

To make a long story short, the first work meeting was set up by telephone. The engineer from Livorno heard Dan's Tuscan accent and didn't think a thing of it.

Two days later they met in Dan's office. They introduced themselves and everything seemed ok: the engineer from Livorno found himself with a young architect that was "a person of color," and like a good Livornese, he tried to deal with his surprise gracefully.

Dan, to his credit, tried to put the engineer at ease by talking about politics, current events, and of course, soccer.

The Livornese engineer wanted to know where Dan had finished his degree and other details about his professional experience. Once reassured, he lavished compliments on my friend, but couldn't hide his surprise over Dan's knowledge of Italian culture and society.

The engineer lamented confidentially to Dan about how the left-wing parties in the government were ruining the country (he supported the idea of "meritocracy" more than the concept of equal rights for all people). He clearly didn't know that Dan was at that time employed as a councilman for one of those left-wing parties.

Once he'd gotten started, the engineer went on about how much you had to work in Italy just to pay taxes.

"It's insane! Just to make it through the year you have to bust your ass working like a nig . . ."

He realized his mistake. Dan started to laugh, and the engineer was in the . . . "blackest" despair.

I FIGLI DI LUCY

I ragazzi all'uscita di scuola si spintonavano scherzosamente. A una spinta più decisa del suo compagno Francesco, Koffi reagì mandandolo a terra sotto le risa del resto della classe:

– Scemo! . . . Stupido! . . . Negro!

Koffi si concentrò e lanciò:

– Negro slavato! . . . Scolorito!

Eh sì . . . in fondo in fondo . . . siamo tutti figli di Lucy!

LUCY'S CHILDREN

School was out for the day and the kids were all jostling and pushing playfully. Francesco got a strong push, so he gave Koffi a stronger push, and Koffi reacted with one strong enough to land Francesco on the ground amid the sound of their classmates' laughter.

Angrily, he cried out, "Dummy! Stupid! *Negro*!"

Koffi concentrated for a minute, then he threw out, "Washed out *Negro*! Colorless!"

Yes, well, ultimately, we are all descendents of Lucy.

PAURA DOPPIA

Vidi la piccola Francesca entrare in sala prelievi, terrorizzata, con i suoi begli occhioni azzurri gonfi di lacrime, strattonata dalla madre:

– Franci, non farmi fare brutta figura! Guarda che è gentile questo dottore . . .

Questo dottore ero io.

Povera bimba, da quando era nata l'avevano sempre ammonita: Se non fai la brava viene l'uomo nero che ti porta via!, oppure: Se non fai la brava chiamo il dottore che ti fa la puntura!

E lì, di colpo, vedendo materializzarsi tutt'e due i suoi incubi in una volta sola, la sua paura non poteva che essere . . . doppia.

Pensai di scherzare per metterla a suo agio:

– Francesca . . . non aver paura, sai . . . ho già mangiato!

Fu allora che scoppiò davvero in un pianto a dirotto.

DOUBLE FEAR

I saw little Francesca in the waiting room, terrified, with her big blue eyes swollen from crying and her mother tugging her along, "Franci, don't embarrass me. Let's just go see the nice doctor."

"The nice doctor" was me.

Poor kid. From the day she was born, they've always warned her, "If you're not good, the big, black man will come and steal you away!" or else, "If you're not good, we'll take you to the doctor and he'll give you a shot!"

Now, right in front of her, both of her worst nightmares had materialized at the same time. No wonder her fear had doubled.

I thought making a joke might put her at ease.

"Don't worry, Francesca, I'm not going to eat you. I've already had lunch."

That's when she *really* started to cry.

OGNI MONDO È PAESE

Quando portammo per la prima volta i nostri figli in Africa a conoscere i nonni paterni, venivano rincorsi e additati dagli altri bambini con grida festose:

– *Yovo! Yovo! Yovo!* (Bianchi!)

I miei pazientarono per i primi giorni ma, siccome la scena si ripeteva di continuo, dovetti spiegare il significato del termine.

Mia figlia, giunti a casa, esasperata mi chiese:

– Papà, perché in Italia mi chiamano negra e qui in Togo mi dicono *Yovo*?

EVERYWHERE YOU GO

When my wife and I took our children to Africa to meet their grandparents for the first time, all the other children ran after them, pointing and shouting excitedly, "Yovo! Yovo! Yovo!" (Whites!)

At first, my children were very patient about it, but since the same scene kept replaying every day, I eventually had to explain what the term meant.

When we got home, one day in frustration, my daughter asked me, "Daddy, why is it that when I'm in Italy, people call me 'black' and when I'm in Togo, they call me 'yovo'?"

LA FORTUNA

Gabri è una bella ragazza metà e metà, cioè di padre italiano e di madre etiope. Quando si presentò per la patente, dopo aver adocchiato con insistenza le sue belle gambe affusolate, l'istruttore, notando che sui documenti c'era scritto: nata ad Addis Abeba, le chiese:

– Come mai ad Addis Abeba?

– Mia madre è etiope!

– Ah sì! Allora sei una mista?

– Sì!

– Che fortunata... quasi non si vede!

Un fortunato angelo travestito da Calimero ruzzolò felicemente nel fango, mentre una voce sciocca e imponente lo rassicurava: Calimero! Calimero! Tu non sei nero, sei solo sporco!

LUCKY

Gabri is a beautiful girl who is "half-and-half," that is, with an Italian father and an Ethiopian mother. When she went to get her driver's license, the administrator of the driving test (after a long stare at her lovely, tapered legs) noticed that on her birth certificate was written, "Born in Addis Ababa." He asked, "Why were you born in Addis Ababa?"

"Because my mother is Ethiopian."

"Oh, so you are half-and-half."

"Yes."

"Wow, how lucky. You can hardly tell."

Just then a lucky angel dressed as Calimero* rolled happily in the mud, while a silly, booming voice reassured him, "Calimero! Calimero! You're not black! You're *only* dirty!"

---

*   Calimero was an animated chick who first appeared on Italian television in the 1960s as part of an advertising campaign for Ava detergent. The chick falls in the mud and isn't recognizable to his mother, but comes clean and returns home thanks to Ava detergent.

NORMALE . . . GELOSIA

Disse la bambina parlando del suo fratellino appena adottato:

– Non mi piace andare in giro con lui, perché lui è anormale.

– Come . . . anormale?

– Sì! Tutti lo guardano perché ha gli occhi così (mimando gli occhi a mandorla) e la pelle scura, invece a me non mi guardano perché io sono normale!

Normale? O, più semplicemente, gelosa?

SIBLING RIVALRY

A little girl was complaining to her mother about the new baby brother their family had just adopted.

"I don't like going outside with the new baby. He's abnormal."

"What do mean, abnormal?"

"He's abnormal! Everyone stares at him because he has eyes like this," (pulling her eyes to a slant) "and his skin is darker and no one even looks at me because I'm only normal!"

Normal? Or maybe just jealous?

KKK

A carnevale, dei colleghi di lavoro invitarono me e la mia dolce metà, di nome e di fatto, a una festa in maschera. Trovammo originale e ironico travestirci, lei, bianca, da schiava nera con le catene, e io, nero, da uomo del famigerato Ku Klux Klan, tutto vestito di bianco con tanto di cappuccio, frusta e guanti.

Appena entrati, la figlia della collega di mia moglie, vedendomi, si mise a urlare spaventata. Mentre tutti ridevano, la madre prese la bambina in braccio e per tranquillizzarla la portò da me dicendole:

– Non aver paura . . . è un amico! E rivolta a me:

– Kossi, togliti quel cappuccio che spaventi mia figlia!

Obbedii all'istante, ma appena la bimba vide la mia faccia nera, trattenne per un attimo il fiato. I suoi occhi si allargarono, la sua faccia diventò paonazza tendente al viola, e infine la sua bocca si spalancò in un urlo infinito.

KKK

At carnival, work colleagues invited me and my better half (in word and deed) to a costume party. We thought it would be unexpected and ironic if we dressed up with her, white, in the chains of a slave, and me, black, as a member of the notorious Ku Klux Klan, white hood and all.

The second we walked through the door, the daughter of one of my wife's colleagues saw me and started to scream. Though everyone laughed, the mother took her child in her arms and, to calm her down, brought her over to me, saying, "Don't be afraid, it's a friend!" and to me, "Kossi, take off that hood, your scaring my daughter!"

I instantly obeyed, but as soon as the child saw my black face, she held her breath for a moment. Then her eyes widened, face flushed purple, and she burst into an endless scream.

CÀ TUA, CÀ MIA, CÀ SUA!

Abeba pestò involontariamente il piede a un *sciur* salendo sull'autobus. Prima di riuscire a scusarsi, si sentì apostrofare:

– Ehi, marocchina di merda, tornatene a *cà tua*! Con calma rispose:

– Vorrei pure tornà a *cà* mia, ma dimmi perché tu, tramite mio padre, invece di stare in Italia a *cà* tua, sei venuto fino in Africa a impollinare mia madre a *cà* sua!

MI CASA ES TU CASA

Abeba accidently stepped on a *gentleman's* foot as she was getting on the bus. Before she even had the chance to apologize, she heard him shout, "Hey, you shit-head Moroccan, get out of *my* country and go back home!"

With great poise, she replied, "I'd like to go back to *my* own home, but first could you tell me how you people, like my Italian father, instead of staying in *your* country, came all the way to Africa to pollenate my mother in *her* home."

DELL'INTEGRAZIONE

Mustafa, tutto felice di aver infine trovato un lavoro, si presentò il primo giorno puntuale in officina. Il caporeparto a cui fu affidato lo accompagnò per presentarlo agli altri operai e spiegargli le sue mansioni.
Strada facendo il capo gli domandò:

    – Tu com'è che ti chiami?

    – Mustafa.

    – Musta . . . Sta . . . troppo complicato, per integrarti bene qua ti ci vuole un nome più semplice . . . come Stefano . . . ecco ti chiameremo . . . Stefano. Ok?

    – . . .

    – Ok?

    – Ok!

INTEGRATION

Mustafa was overjoyed at having found a job and reported to work early the first day. The manager was showing him around, introducing him to the other employees, and explaining his responsibilities.

Along the way, the manager asked, "So what's your name again?"

"Mustafa."

"Musta. . sta. . . that's really complicated. Look, if you want to fit in here, you're going to need a name that's easier to remember. Something easier like . . . Stefano. That's it. We're going to call you Stefano, got it?"

" . . . "

"Ok?"

"Ok."

LA MARCIA DELLA PACE

Il mio amico Miguel, angolano, è felicemente sposato da anni con una ragazza del sud, dove abitano. Unico tormento: ogni volta che passeggiano per le strade della città, lui inorridisce nel sentire i vergognosi nomignoli che alcuni energumeni lanciano verso la consorte.

– Pensare che da noi è quasi un orgoglio aver sposato una bianca, mentre qui ti danno della puttana per aver sposato un nero!

Decisero di comune accordo di ignorarli chiudendosi in uno sprezzante silenzio.

Una sera, andando a cena da amici, si sorbirono lungo il cammino tutto un repertorio di *begli* aggettivi. Miguel era così esasperato che quando a fine pasto i loro amici chiesero loro di aderire alla marcia della pace che stavano organizzando, rispose con rabbia mista ad amarezza:

– Ehi no! Grazie! Noi facciamo tutti i santi giorni la marcia per la pace!

PEACE MARCH

My friend Miguel from Angola is happily married to a woman from southern Italy, where they now live. But there's a constant problem: every time they go out out for a walk, he's outraged when he hears the insults that the local punks yell at his wife:

"Just think, where I'm from it's almost a point of pride to marry a white woman, but here they call her a whore for having married *un nero*."

Miguel and his wife decided together to ignore all comments and respond with silence.

One evening, walking across town on their way to have dinner with friends, they suffered through the whole repetoire of those "nice" adjectives from bystanders. When their friends asked them at the end of the meal if they'd be willing to join in the peace march they were organizing, Miguel was still so exasperated. He couldn't hide the sarcasm when he said, "No, thanks. Every day we go through our own peace march!"

DELLA NEGRITUDINE

La piccola Larissa scoppiò in lacrime tornando da scuola:

– Mamma, io non sono negra!

– Come, figlia mia?

– Io non voglio essere negra.

– Ma tu sei negra!

– No!

– Ma perché fai così?

– Una compagna in classe mi ha detto: Stai zitta, negra!

– Vedi, Larissa: papà è nero e la mamma è nera, quindi anche tu sei nera!

– Sì, mamma . . . ma io non voglio essere negra!

Un angelo nero passò con uno specchio infranto, raccogliendo spine.

NEGRITUDE

Little Larissa came home from school crying.

"Mama, I'm not black!"

"What on earth do you mean, sweetheart?"

"I mean I don't want to be black."

"But, honey, you are black."

"No!"

"What's wrong?"

"A girl in class said, 'Shut up, you nigger!'"

"Larissa, your father is black, and I am black, too, so of course you're black."

"I know, Mama, but . . . I don't want to be!"

A black angel passed with a shattered mirror, gathering thorns.

AMATEVI GLI UNI GLI ALTRI,
o meglio: TEMPI NUOVI VERRANNO

Alla messa per la festa dei popoli, durante l'omelia, l'arcivescovo salì in cattedra per ringraziare la comunità straniera per il ritmo gioioso dei loro canti, poi supplicò:

– Le nostre case, i nostri figli e i nostri anziani sono nelle vostre mani... vi chiedo di non prendervela con loro, se vi trattiamo male... curateli bene . . . amateli!

Finita la celebrazione, si rifiutò di andare a salutare sul sagrato i giovani della comunità musulmana, venuti a rendergli omaggio:

– I tempi non sono ancora maturi –, disse.

LOVE ONE ANOTHER,
OR BETTER YET: NEW TIMES ARE COMING

At the mass celebrated during the "Festival of All Peoples,"* the archbishop went up to the ambo for his homily. He thanked the congregation of foreigners for their lively participation in the singing, then he remonstrated, "You take care of our houses, you watch our children and our elderly, they're in your hands, so we ask you, please be patient and don't be upset if they treat you badly . . . always take good care of them, and love them!"

At the end of the ceremony, he refused to go to the sacristy and shake hands with the youth of the Muslim community who had come to meet him because, he explained, "The time for that is not yet come."

---

* The "Festa dei Popoli" began in 1991, and is a festival held annually in Padova celebrating cultural diversity. It's purpose is to promote contact and understanding between different groups and ethnicities.

NERO NATALE

Matteo, un bel giovane di origine africana, aveva appena assistito alla messa della notte di Natale insieme a suo padre adottivo, italiano. Mentre questi si tratteneva per salutare alcuni conoscenti, il giovane si avviò verso il sagrato fermandosi poi ad aspettarlo.

Un'anziana signora, entrando in chiesa, gli mise in mano una moneta di due euro:

– Buon Natale!

Sbalordito, Matteo fissò pensoso la moneta, con la fronte corrugata. Poi, con un sorriso divertito, se l'infilò in tasca.

Un angelo nero, con due occhioni così, la pancia gonfia di fame e i capelli diradati, si accarezzò le costole sporgenti rassegnato e le contò fischiettando: Bianco Natale!

BLACK CHRISTMAS

Matteo, a young man of African descent, went to midnight mass on Christmas Eve with his adoptive father, who is Italian. While his father visited with some acquaintances, the young man waited in the sacristy.

On her way out of the church after the service, an elderly woman slid a 2 Euro coin into Matteo's hand and whispered, "Merry Christmas!"

Speechless, Matteo stared thoughtfully at the coin with a furrowed brow. Then with a smile, he slipped it into his pocket.

Just then, a black angel with two enormous eyes and its stomach bloated from malnutrition, its hair sparse and limp, counted the ribs poking from its sides as it whistled, "White Christmas."

VENDETTA NERA

Una sera, mentre lei era al lavoro, dei ladri provarono a entrare in casa di Gabri, una mia amica italo-etiope di carnagione chiara. L'indomani, vedendo infranto il vetro esterno della finestra, si accorse dell'accaduto. Sul pianerottolo incontrò una vicina che glielo confermò:

– È stata fortunata: se non fosse per l'anziana signora del piano di sopra, che si è sporta dal balcone e li ha cacciati via minacciandoli di chiamare la polizia, i ladri le sarebbero entrati in casa.

Riconoscente, dopo qualche giorno si presentò dalla sua salvatrice con una pianta per ringraziarla. Quella rispose:

– Ah! Non so neanche con che coraggio l'ho fatto, mi è venuto istintivo, non ho neanche pensato che potesse essere uno di quei negri... sa, quelli non hanno scrupoli: ti aspettano e poi, appena giri l'angolo, si vendicano!

REVENGE

My friend Gabri is Italian-Ethiopian, and has a very light complexion. One night while she was at work, burglars tried to break into her house. She realized what had happened the next day when she found a back window broken in and glass scattered everywhere. She later met a neighbor lady on the landing who confirmed her fears, "You were really lucky: the elderly lady who lives above you saw someone trying to break in, and she leaned out of her balcony and shouted that she was going to call the police. If it hadn't been for her, you could have been robbed!"

Gratefully, Gabri went to visit her elderly defender, and took a plant to thank her.

The elderly neighbor confided, "Oh, I don't know if I was brave or not. I just saw someone and thought, it could've been one of those *negri*! You know the kind, the ones that have no morals. They wait for you and then when you turn the corner, they take revenge on you somehow!"

CUORE DI NONNA

– Sai Koffi –, confidò imbarazzata, dopo anni, la nonna italiana al nipote adottato – quando eri piccolo, appena arrivato, continuavo a insaponarti e a lavarti le mani di nascosto perché credevo fossero . . . sporche.

A GRANDMOTHER'S LOVE

After he was grown, Koffi's Italian grandmother confessed to her adopted grandson with embarrassment, "You know, when you were a baby and we'd just gotten you, when no one was looking, I used to lather and rinse your hands all the time in secret because I was sure that they were just . . . dirty."

PARLA 'ME TA MÀNGET

Durante il giro mattutino in reparto, entrando in una stanza, il primario si rivolse con aria professionale alla *sciüra* Maria Bambina (anni 74) del letto 124, e guardando la sua cartella disse:

– Signora, lei ha una distorsione di primo grado al ginocchio destro con un lieve interessamento dei legamenti collaterali esterni, fortunatamente senza lesioni meniscali e soprattutto senza coinvolgimenti dei crociati. Inoltre . . .

Man mano che lui andava avanti, vedevo la signora sgranare gli occhi sempre più terrorizzata.

Stavamo per passare nella stanza accanto quando d'istinto mi fermai per tornare sui miei passi e chiedere alla paziente:

– *Nona, l'ha capii quell ca la dii ul Dutur?*

– *Mé ho capii propi nagòtt.*

– *Sciüra, gal dissi mé quell ch'è suceduu: se la stramba ul ginöcc!*

– Ah! –, fece lei visibilmente sollevata alla vista di un brianzolo . . . nero.

"PARLA 'ME TA MANGET'"*

During his morning rounds, the attending physician went in to room 124 and with a professional air and a glance at her chart, said to *sciüra*** Maria Bambina, 74 years old, "Ma'am, you have sustained a level-one torsion to your right knee with some damage to the external collateral ligaments, fortunately without any lesions on the meniscus or above all, without any damage to the connective tissue. Furthermore . . ."

He noticed his patient's eyes gradually growing larger in increasing terror . . .

We were just about to move on to the next room when instinctively I turned around asked the patient, "*Nona, l'ha capii quell ca la dii ul Dutur?*" ("Granny, did you understand what that doctor said to you?")

"*Mè ho capii propri nagòtt.*" ("No, not a word.")

"*Sciura, gal dissi mè quell ch'è suceduu: se la stramba ul ginocc!*" ("I'll tell you what he said: you banged up your knee!")

"Oooh!" she said, visibly relieved to see someone (black) from Brianzolo.

---

* Dialect form of "parla come mangi," or "talk to me straight."
** Dialect form of "Signora."

FRUTTAIDS

Sapete cosa dice la madre dell'amica di Gabri quando si mangia la frutta senza lavarla?

– Guarda che l'hanno raccolta i negri con tutto quell'AIDS!

FRUTTAIDS

Do you know what Gabri's mother says if some one tries to eat a piece of fruit without washing it first?

"Be careful! Don't you know that the *negri* who picked it all have AIDS?"

TIFO . . . DI COLORE

Un'estate, eravamo al mare in un villaggio turistico durante i mondiali di calcio.

La sera dell'incontro Italia-Brasile, mio figlio, tifoso sfegatato degli azzurri e interista doc (cioè sfigato), non stava più nella pelle. Da buon italiano, soffriva, criticava, esultava, imprecava contro l'arbitro, consigliava l'allenatore e suggeriva i passaggi ai giocatori. A un certo punto, gli si avvicinò un altro bambino per chiedergli:

– Perché fai il tifo per l'Italia?

– Perché, non posso fare il tifo per l'Italia?

– No! Tu devi fare il tifo per il Brasile!

– Ma perché?

THE COLOR OF A SOCCER FAN

One summer we were at a seaside hotel during the World Cup.

The night of the Italy v. Brazil game, my son, who is a fanatical fan of the Italian Azzurri team and a staunch (or rather, cursed) Interista supporter, was jumping out of his skin with excitement. In perfect Italian, he cried, criticized, rejoiced, insulted the referee, advised the coaches, and told the players what to do.

After a while, a boy came up to my son and asked, "Why are you rooting for Italy?"

"Why can't I be rooting for Italy?"

"No! You have to root for Brazil."

"But why?"

LA PECORA ... NERA

Matteo, un giovane di origine togolese, mi raccontava: Tornavamo dalla Francia col TGV io e Franco, un mio amico italiano. Nella nostra carrozza c'erano gruppi di giovani un po' chiassosi e in vena di scherzi. A un certo punto, iniziarono a produrre il rumore della scoreggia con un sacchetto giocattolo. Andarono avanti così per circa tre quarti d'ora, e la cosa diventava davvero fastidiosa e irritante. Mi dicevo che qualcuno doveva intervenire per farli smettere, ma non volevo fare io la parte del guastafeste. Proprio mentre stavo comunicando questo pensiero al mio amico, mi passò accanto nel corridoio una signora, e in quello stesso momento risuonò il malefico rumore. La donna si girò di scatto verso di me e in tono cattivo mi aggredì:

– Non siamo mica in una stalla!

Un angelo ... nero dalla vergogna, testa e occhi bassi, se la svignò alla chetichella ... otturandosi il naso.

THE . . . BLACK SHEEP

Matteo, a young Togolese friend told me about coming back from France on the TGV Train with his Italian friend, Franco.

Matteo explained, "Our compartment was filled with a group of rowdy kids who were horsing around. They started making farting sounds with a whoopee cushion, and kept it up for about 45 minutes. This was all getting pretty irritating. I was thinking how somebody should make them quit it, but I didn't want to play the heavy. I was sharing this thought with a friend when I noticed a woman walking down the train's corridor, and just as she walked passed our compartment, the kids set off the whoopee cushion. She whipped around and jumped at *me*, 'This isn't a stable, you know!'"

Just then an angel, *black with shame*, head bowed and eyes downcast slunk away, holding his nose.

INNOCENTE CURIOSITÀ

Durante un incontro sulla favolistica africana coi bambini dell'asilo, notai una bambina molto in disparte. Pian piano, sul finire della mattinata, presa confidenza, la piccola mi si era avvicinata. Io continuavo a raccontare la mia favola, quando notai con la coda dell'occhio che mi accarezzava la mano con l'indice.

Poi, ignara di essere osservata, si guardò il lato del dito alla ricerca di una traccia di colore. Ripeté l'esperimento passandosi il dito sulla pelle, ma niente. Infine, dovette concludere con disappunto che non ero fatto di cioccolato perché perse ogni interesse nei miei riguardi.

INNOCENT CURIOSITY

During one of my presentations about African fables at a preschool, I noticed that one little girl kept far away. Slowly, toward the end of the morning, the girl grew braver and came over to me. I continued telling my stories when out of the corner of my eye, I caught the little girl surreptitiously stroking my hand with her finger.

Then, unaware of being observed, she looked at her finger, searching for a trace of color. She repeated this experiment again, rubbing her finger against my skin. I think she finally concluded disappointedly that I wasn't made of chocolate because she then lost all interest in me and my stories.

IL CELLULARE

Alessandro e la sua giovane moglie nigeriana andarono all'ufficio postale per riscuotere un vaglia. Alex entrò da solo e, una volta allo sportello, mise il cellulare a portata di mano. Non vedendolo tornare, la moglie decise di entrare a sua volta, e, avvicinatasi al marito, allungò le mani verso il telefonino. Subito l'impiegato si sporse in avanti per sussurrare ad Alex:

– Stia attento a quella ladra di una negra, le sta fregando il cellulare!

– Chi? Mia moglie?

Un angelo con le spalle ricurve, paonazzo e boccheggiante, cercò di sprofondare in un pacco prima di farsi spedire al diavolo per posta prioritaria.

CELL PHONE

Alessandro and his young Nigerian wife went to the post office to redeem a money order. Alex went in alone, stopped at the counter to write something, and set his cell phone on the counter beside him. When he didn't come out of the post office, his wife went in after him. She'd just found her husband and reached out for their phone. Immediately, the clerk leaned forward and whispered to Alex, "Watch out! That black thief is trying to rip off your cell phone!"

"Who? My wife?"

Just then an angel with bent wings, flushed and out of breath, tried to disappear inside a package before shipping itself to the devil, first-class.

L'AMORE . . . ANORMALE

Il mio amico senegalese Pap chiese a sua moglie, italiana, di raccontargli la trama del film che era andata a vedere.

– È la storia di una coppia: lei normale e lui gitano che . . .

– Come? Non ho capito!

– È la storia di una coppia. Lei è una normale, cioè italiana, e lui è un gitano. Hai capito?

– Lei normale! Certo che ho capito: quindi fra me e te io sarei l'anormale e tu la normale! Vero?

STRANGE LOVE

My Senegalese friend, Pap, asked his Italian wife to tell him about the movie she'd gone to see.

"Well, it was a love story. She was normal and he was a gypsy who . . ."

"What? I don't understand."

"It's the story of couple. She was normal, you know, Italian, and he was a gypsy. You get it?"

"She was normal! Ok, I think I get it: just like you and me. You're normal and I'm the freak?"

FIGLI BIOLOGICI – FIGLI ADOTTIVI

Giulio e Paola, due italiani, erano sdraiati in spiaggia con una coppia di amici mentre le loro rispettive figlie—Eva, la bionda, figlia adottiva di Giulio e Paola, e Ester, la meticcia, figlia di Kamanda e Maria Rosa —erano a giocare in riva al mare.

Due signore, ignare di passare vicino ai genitori, commentarono:

– Come stanno bene insieme quelle bambine!

– Bella la morettina!

– Sì, proprio bella . . . l'avranno adottata!

BIOLOGICAL CHILDREN, ADOPTED CHILDREN

Giulio and Paola, both Italian, were stretched out on the beach with their friends Kamanda and Maria Rosa, a "mixed" couple. Their respective children—Giulio and Paola's little blonde daughter, adopted from the Ukraine, and Esther, the "mixed race" daughter of Kamanda and Maria Rosa—played together in the water.

Two women walking past the parents, oblivious to the actual relationships, commented, "Look how cute those little girls are, playing together!"

"Ah, that little dark one is especially cute!"

"Yeah, she's really pretty. They must have adopted her."

IL DUBBIO ALL'ESAME D'ITALIANITÀ

– Conosci le parolacce in italiano?

    – Sì.

    – Dimmene una!

    – Extracomunitario!

    – Ma dai! Anche gli svizzeri e gli americani sono extracomunitari!

    – Quindi non è una parolaccia?

    – Certo che no!

    – Anche se ci definisce per quello che non siamo?

    – Sì.

    – Allora spiegami perché un ragazzino di quattordici anni, solo perché è nato in Italia, mi ha dato dell'extracomunitario, a me che sono in Italia da ormai trent'anni, lavoro, pago le tasse, mi sono ingozzato di chili di spaghetti e pizza, mi sono sorbito tutti i festival di Sanremo, gli scioperi, le crisi di governo, le code, ho tifato per gli azzurri e per di più ho la cittadinanza italiana, sono sposato con un'italiana e ho figli italiani? . . . Forse perché sono nero?

    – . . .

ITALIANNESS TEST

"Do you know any swear words in Italian?"

"Yes."

"Well, tell me one."

"*Extracommunitario!* "*

"Really? So even Americans and Swiss are *extracommunitari* for you?"

"Then it's not a swear word?"

"Of course not!"

"But don't we define ourselves by what we are *not* ?"

"Yes."

"Then could someone please explain to me why a 14-year old boy, simply because he was born in Italy, can call me '*extracommunitario?* ' I, who have lived in this country for more than 30 years; I, who have worked, paid taxes, and ingested pound after pound of spaghetti and pizza; for all these years, I have suffered through every musical Festival of Sanremo, the strikes, the government crises, the long lines, I have cheered for the national soccer team, and I even have Italian citizenship, I'm married to an Italian woman, and have Italian children? Perhaps, could it be because I'm black?"

---

* "Extracommunitario" literally means a person from outside of the European Union, but is a term typically and pejoratively applied to migrants of color.

RINGRAZIAMENTI

I miei più sinceri ringraziamenti vanno a tutti coloro i quali, da vicino o da lontano, hanno partecipato alla realizzazione di questa versione inglese dei miei *Imbarazzismi*. In particolare vorrei ricordare

L'onorevole Cécile Kyenge, Past Italian Minister of Integration per la prefazione alla versione italiana

La professoressa Marie Orton della Brigham Young University. Senza la sua tenace determinazione a volerlo tradurre questo testo non avrebbe mai visto la luce.

Graziella Parati, the Paul D. Paganucci Professor of Italian at Dartmouth College per la sua generosa e affettuosa introduzione.

Il Prof. John A. Powell University of California at Berkely. Il suo autorevole endorsment ha certamente contribuito a dare rilievo e risonanza a questa opera.

L'amico Prof. Peter N. Pedroni della Miami University e suo figlio Associate Professor Thomas C. Pedroni Wayne State University per il loro sostegno e disponibilità.

Da ultimo ma non per importanza un sentito grazie al Co-Director Anthony J. Tamburri and Nicholas Grosso della Bordighera Press per la loro totale convinzione e professionalità che hanno reso questo mio sogno realtà.

A tutti la mia più profonda gratitudine.

ACKNOWLEDGEMENTS

My sincere thanks go to all those who, from near and far, have been part of bringing about the English language version of *Imbarazzismi*. I especially wish to acknowledge:

The Honorable Cécile Kyenge, Former Italian Minister of Integration, for her preface to the Italian edition of the book.

Professor Marie Orton of Brigham Young University. Without her tenacious determination to see this text translated, it would never have seen the light of day.

Graziella Parati, Paul D. Paganucci Professor of Italian at Dartmouth College, for her warm and generous introduction.

Professor John A. Powell from the University of California at Berkely. His authoritative endorsement has certainly expanded the reach and awareness of this work.

My friend Professor Peter N. Pedroni of Miami University and his son Associate Professor Thomas C. Pedroni of Wayne State University for their willing support and help.

Last on the list but not last in importance, a heart-felt thank you to co-director Anthony Tamburri and Nicholas Grosso of Bordighera Press. Their utter commitment and professionalism have made my dream a reality.

My deepest thanks to all of you.

ABOUT THE AUTHOR

KOSSI AMÉKOWOYOA KOMLA-EBRI (10 January 1954) is a doctor and writer born in Tsévié, Togo. He is the winner of the 2005 Premio Mare Nostrum for Literature and the 2009 Premio Graphein awarded by Società di Pedagogia e Didattica della Scrittura. He lives in Como.

ABOUT THE TRANSLATOR

Marie Orton is professor of Italian at Brigham Young University. She holds a Ph.D. from the University of Chicago and her research focuses on issues of migration. Her translation work includes an anthology of prose writings by seventeen migrant authors in Italy co-edited with Graziella Parati, *Multicultural Literature in Contemporary Italy* (2007), as well as a sociological study, *Non-Persons: The Exclusion of Migrants in a Global Society* by Alessandro Dal Lago (2008). Her forthcoming and ongoing translation projects include Edmondo de Amicis' novel, *Across the Ocean*, and Monica Miniati's historical study, *Le "emancipate": le donne ebree in Italia nel XIX e XX secolo.*

CROSSINGS

AN INTERSECTION OF CULTURES

Crossings is dedicated to the publication of Italian-language literature and translations from Italian to English.

Rodolfo Di Biasio
> *Wayfarers Four*. Translated by Justin Vitello. 1998. ISBN 1-88419-17-9. Vol 1.

Isabella Morra
> *Canzoniere: A Bilingual Edition*. Translated by Irene Musillo Mitchell. 1998. ISBN 1-88419-18-6. Vol 2.

Nevio Spadone
> *Lus*. Translated by Teresa Picarazzi. 1999. ISBN 1-88419-22-4. Vol 3.

Flavia Pankiewicz
> *American Eclipses*. Translated by Peter Carravetta. Introduction by Joseph Tusiani. 1999. ISBN 1-88419-23-2. Vol 4.

Dacia Maraini
> *Stowaway on Board*. Translated by Giovanna Bellesia and Victoria Offredi Poletto. 2000. ISBN 1-88419-24-0. Vol 5.

Walter Valeri, editor
> *Franca Rame: Woman on Stage*. 2000. ISBN 1-88419-25-9. Vol 6.

Carmine Biagio Iannace
> *The Discovery of America*. Translated by William Boelhower. 2000. ISBN 1-88419-26-7. Vol 7.

Romeo Musa da Calice
> *Luna sul salice*. Translated by Adelia V. Williams. 2000. ISBN 1-88419-39-9. Vol 8.

Marco Paolini & Gabriele Vacis
> *The Story of Vajont*. Translated by Thomas Simpson. 2000. ISBN 1-88419-41-0. Vol 9.

Silvio Ramat
> *Sharing A Trip: Selected Poems*. Translated by Emanuel di Pasquale. 2001. ISBN 1-88419-43-7. Vol 10.

Raffaello Baldini
> *Page Proof*. Edited by Daniele Benati. Translated by Adria Bernardi. 2001. ISBN 1-88419-47-X. Vol 11.

Maura Del Serra
  Infinite Present. Translated by Emanuel di Pasquale and
  Michael Palma. 2002. ISBN 1-88419-52-6. Vol 12.

Dino Campana
  Canti Orfici. Translated and Notes by Luigi Bonaffini. 2003.
  ISBN 1-88419-56-9. Vol 13.

Roberto Bertoldo
  The Calvary of the Cranes. Translated by Emanuel di Pasquale.
  2003. ISBN 1-88419-59-3. Vol 14.

Paolo Ruffilli
  Like It or Not. Translated by Ruth Feldman and James Laughlin.
  2007. ISBN 1-88419-75-5. Vol 15.

Giuseppe Bonaviri
  Saracen Tales. Translated Barbara De Marco. 2006. ISBN
  1-88419-76-3. Vol 16.

Leonilde Frieri Ruberto
  Such Is Life. Translated Laura Ruberto. Introduction by Ilaria
  Serra. 2010. ISBN 978-1-59954-004-7. Vol 17.

Gina Lagorio
  Tosca the Cat Lady. Translated by Martha King. 2009. ISBN 978-
  1-59954-002-3. Vol 18.

Marco Martinelli
  Rumore di acque. Translated and edited by Thomas Simpson.
  2014. ISBN 978-1-59954-066-5. Vol 19.

Emanuele Pettener
  A Season in Florida. Translated by Thomas De Angelis. 2014.
  ISBN 978-1-59954-052-2. Vol 20.

Angelo Spina
  Il cucchiaio trafugato. 2017. ISBN 978-1-59954-112-9. Vol 21.

Michela Zanarella
  Meditations in the Feminine. Translated by Leanne Hoppe. 2017.
  ISBN 978-1-59954-110-5. Vol 22.

Francesco "Kento" Carlo
  Resistenza Rap. Translated by Emma Gainsforth and Siân
  Gibby. 2017. ISBN 978-1-59954-112-9. Volume 23.